YORK N

York Notes Rapid Revision

Macbeth

AQA GCSE English Literature

Written by Susannah White

 Pearson

YORK PRESS
322 Old Brompton Road, London SW5 9JH

PEARSON EDUCATION LIMITED
80 Strand, London, WC2R 0RL

10 9 8 7 6 5 4 3 2 1

ISBN 978–1–2922–7087–6

Phototypeset by Kamae Design
Printed in Slovakia

Photo credits:
LifetimeStock/Shutterstock for page 3 bottom, 24 bottom and 38 bottom / Neiro Photo/ Shutterstock for page 4 top and page 28 top / Olena Zaskochenko/Shutterstock for page 6 middle and page 32 top / M Kunz/Shutterstock for page 8 middle / Tereshchenko Dmitry/Shutterstock for page 10 middle and page 34 top / John Kellerman/Alamy for page 12 middle / Tetra Images LLC/ Alamy for page 14 bottom and 36 bottom / Aggie 11/Shutterstock for page 16 bottom and page 46 middle / Neiron Photo/Shutterstock for page 18 bottom and page 30 top / Ilbusca/Betty Images for page 22 bottom and 50 bottom / Johan Swanepoel/Shutterstock for page 26 middle / Ilaszio/ Shutterstock for page 26 bottom / Lorado/© iStock for page 36 top / quruXOX/Shutterstock for page 38 bottom / Everett Collection/Alamy for page 40 top / Lawrey/Shutterstock for page 44 middle / Evgeny Pyatkov/Shutterstock for page 48 top / Kanuman/Shutterstock for page 52 middle / Melinda Fawyer/Shutterstock for page 54 bottom / Fauzan Maududdin/Shutterstock for page 58 bottom / neko92vl/© iStock for page 60 middle

CONTENTS

PLOT AND STRUCTURE

Act I Scenes 1–4	4
Act I Scenes 5–7	6
Act II	8
Act III Scenes 1–3	10
Act III Scenes 4–6	12
Act IV	14
Act V	16
Form and structure	18
Quick revision	20

SETTING AND CONTEXT

Jacobean society	22
Succession and order	24
Settings	26

CHARACTERS

Macbeth in Acts I and II	28
Macbeth in Acts III–V	30
Lady Macbeth	32
Banquo	34
Macduff and Lady Macduff	36
King Duncan and Malcolm	38
The witches	40
Quick revision	42

THEMES

Ambition	44
Betrayal and revenge	46
The supernatural	48
Fate and free will	50
Appearance and reality	52
Guilt and madness	54
Quick revision	56

LANGUAGE

Imagery and symbolism	58
Dramatic techniques	60

EXAM PRACTICE

Understanding the exam	62
Character questions	64
Planning your character response	66
Grade 5 annotated sample answer	68
Grade 7+ annotated sample answer	70
Theme questions	72
Planning your theme response	74
Grade 5 annotated sample answer	76
Grade 7+ annotated sample answer	78
Practice questions	80

GLOSSARY 82

ANSWERS 83

3

PLOT AND STRUCTURE Act I Scenes 1-4

Three key things about Act I Scenes 1-4

1. The play opens with **three witches** out in a **storm**.
2. We meet **Macbeth**, a **brave warrior**, who appears to be **loyal to King Duncan**.
3. Key **themes** are introduced: the **supernatural**, **ambition**, **violent conflict** and **appearance and reality**.

What happens in Scenes 1-2?

- **Scene 1:** Three witches appear and arrange to meet Macbeth.
- They refer to a **'battle'** and **'hurly-burly'**, suggesting that conflict is raging all around them.
- **Scene 2:** An army captain informs King Duncan that Macbeth and his friend, Banquo, fought courageously in a battle against the king's enemies.
- He also reports that Macbeth fought ruthlessly because he **'unseamed'** their enemy, Macdonald, then fixed his severed head on the battlements.

What happens in Scenes 3-4?

- **Scene 3:** Macbeth and fellow soldier, Banquo meet the witches who hail Macbeth as **'Thane of Cawdor'** and **'king hereafter'** and tell Banquo that his sons will be kings.
- One of the witches' prophecies comes true immediately when King Duncan makes Macbeth Thane of Cawdor as a reward for his loyalty and courage.
- Banquo warns Macbeth about the witches, claiming that the **'instruments of darkness'** sometimes tell truths in order to cause harm.
- **Scene 4:** We learn that the previous Thane of Cawdor, a man who betrayed King Duncan's **'absolute trust'** has been executed.
- King Duncan names Malcolm, his eldest son, as his heir.
- Macbeth concludes he will need to **'o'erleap'** Malcolm in order to become king as the witches predicted.

Five key quotations

1. The theme of appearance and reality: 'Fair is foul, and foul is fair' (witches) (I.1.12)

2. Macbeth's reputation: 'For brave Macbeth – well he deserves that name' (Captain) (I.2.16)

3. Macbeth's violent conduct: 'his brandish'd steel,/Which smok'd with bloody execution' (Captain) (I.2.16–17)

4. Macbeth's evil side: 'Stars, hide your fires,/Let not light see my black and deep desires' (I.4.50–1)

5. Macbeth's interest in the supernatural: 'Stay, you imperfect speakers. Tell me more' (I.3.68)

Note it!

Note how Act I Scene 1 grabs our attention: stormy weather, the witches' chanting and their contradictory riddles create a mysterious atmosphere. Their final chant **'Fair is foul, and foul is fair'** resembles Macbeth's first words: **'So foul and fair a day I have not seen'**, linking him with them.

Exam focus

How can I write about Macbeth?

You can focus on Scenes 1 and 2 to show how Shakespeare introduces Macbeth.

> At the beginning of Act I, we hear about Macbeth twice before we see him. Firstly, in Scene 1, three witches plan to meet him, which gives us the impression that Macbeth is associated with witchcraft. Then, in Scene 2, the Captain reveals how 'brave Macbeth' fought courageously in battle. Both these reported references to Macbeth raise the audience's curiosity and build up expectations before his appearance.

Clear topic sentence to introduce paragraph

Analytical comment showing effect

Quotation used to illustrate point

Explanation and development of main point

Now you try!

Finish this paragraph about Macbeth. Use one of the quotations from the list.

Shakespeare also reveals other aspects of Macbeth's character in the early scenes of Act I. One of these aspects is his evil side which is evident when ....

Three key things about Act I Scenes 5-7

1. The **action moves** to Macbeth's castle at **Inverness**.
2. We meet **Lady Macbeth**: a **strong, ambitious** woman who has a **close relationship** with her husband.
3. The key **themes** of **ambition** and **good and evil** are developed.

What happens in Scenes 5-6?

- **Scene 5:** Lady Macbeth reads a letter from Macbeth about the witches' prophecies.
- She asks dark spirits to **'unsex'** her and fill her with **'direst cruelty'** so she can persuade Macbeth to murder King Duncan.
- When Macbeth arrives, the couple discuss the murder plan and Lady Macbeth takes charge of the arrangements.
- **Scene 6:** King Duncan, Banquo and other royal attendants arrive and comment on the **'pleasant'** setting of Macbeth's castle and the **'delicate'** air surrounding it.
- Lady Macbeth welcomes King Duncan, playing the role of the perfect hostess.

What happens in Scene 7?

- Macbeth wrestles with his conscience because he knows that as King Duncan's host he should protect him from danger, not **'bear the knife'** against him.
- He acknowledges that **'Vaulting ambition'** is his only reason for murdering the king.
- After much deliberation, Macbeth tells Lady Macbeth that he will not proceed with the murder.
- Lady Macbeth questions her husband's courage and manliness in order to persuade him to kill King Duncan. She convinces him to go ahead with the murder.
- The couple decide to smear the two grooms guarding King Duncan with blood when they are asleep so that they will be blamed for the murder.

Five key quotations

1. The relationship between Macbeth and his wife: 'my dearest partner of greatness' (Macbeth) (I.5.10)
2. Lady Macbeth's links to evil: 'fill me from the crown to the toe topfull/ Of direst cruelty' (I.5.41–2)
3. Lady Macbeth's view of Macbeth: 'too full o'th'milk of human kindness' (I.5.16)
4. The theme of good and evil: 'his virtues/ Will plead like angels, trumpet-tongu'd against/The deep damnation of his taking-off' (Macbeth) (I.7.18–20)
5. The theme of ambition: 'Glamis thou art, and Cawdor, and shalt be/What thou art promis'd' (Lady Macbeth) (I.7.14–15)

Note it!

Lady Macbeth never uses the word 'murder' when she discusses killing King Duncan with Macbeth. Instead she says Duncan must be **'provided for'** and speaks of the **'night's great business'**. Her words are deliberately euphemistic and could refer to making the necessary preparations for Duncan's visit.

Exam focus

How can I write about good and evil?

You can show how Shakespeare portrays the good and evil traits of his characters.

> In Act I Scene 7, Shakespeare uses his characters to introduce the theme of good and evil. When Macbeth contemplates murdering the virtuous King Duncan, he fears that Duncan's goodness will be magnified by his death since memories of his virtues will plead 'like angels' against the crime. This simile connects Duncan with heaven and reminds us that, in Jacobean times, some people, including King James I, believed that the king was appointed by God.

Clear topic sentence to introduce paragraph

Relevant embedded quotation

Analytical comment with effect

Link to historical context

Now you try!

Finish this paragraph about good and evil. Use one of the quotations from the list.

Shakespeare further explores the concept of evil in the second half of Act I when Lady Macbeth ....

Three key things about Act II

1. **Act II** begins **inside Macbeth's castle**, in the **middle of the night**.
2. Macbeth's **conscience** is troubled **before** and **after** King Duncan's murder.
3. Key **motifs** are explored: **blood, water** and **sleep**.

What happens in Scene 1?

- Banquo gives Macbeth a diamond for Lady Macbeth from King Duncan.
- Banquo tells Macbeth that he dreamt about the witches but Macbeth claims he does not think of them.
- Macbeth seems to test Banquo's support but Banquo says he will keep his **'allegiance clear'**.
- Macbeth thinks he sees a dagger leading him towards King Duncan's chamber. A bell rings as he goes to kill Duncan.

What happens in Scene 2?

- Lady Macbeth waits nervously for Macbeth.
- Macbeth appears carrying two bloody daggers. He is distressed and claims that he heard a voice saying **'Sleep no more'**.
- Lady Macbeth takes control, returns the daggers and smears the grooms with blood. She claims **'A little water'** will wash away the deed.
- They hear knocking and hurry to bed.

What happens in Scenes 3-4?

- **Scene 3:** The porter opens the door to two noblemen: Macduff and Lennox.
- Macduff discovers Duncan's body.
- Macbeth claims the grooms killed Duncan and that he then killed them in anger.
- The king's sons, Malcolm and Donaldbain, flee for their lives.
- **Scene 4:** Ross, another nobleman, and an old man discuss disturbances in nature.
- Macbeth prepares for his coronation but Macduff decides not to attend.

Five key quotations

1. Macbeth's vision: 'art thou but/A dagger of the mind, a false creation,/ Proceeding from the heat-oppressed brain?' (II.1.37–9)

2. The motif of sleep: 'Methought I heard a voice cry, "Sleep no more:/ Macbeth does murder sleep"' (Macbeth) (II.2.38–9)

3. The motifs of blood and water: 'Will all great Neptune's ocean wash this blood/Clean from my hand?' (Macbeth) (II.2.63–4)

4. Lady Macbeth taking control: 'Infirm of purpose!/Give me the daggers' (II.2.55–6)

5. The motif of disturbance in the natural world: 'On Tuesday last,/A falcon tow'ring in her pride of place/Was by a mousing owl hawk'd at and kill'd' (Old Man) (II.4.11–13)

Note it!

The Porter, who is unwell after drinking too much the previous night, provides a comic interlude between King Duncan's murder and the discovery of his body. The humour is offset when he describes the castle's entrance as a **'hell-gate'**, which reminds us of the horrors within and links Macbeth to the Devil.

Exam focus

How can I write about motifs? AO2

You can write about how Shakespeare uses key motifs in Act II.

> Shakespeare includes several key motifs in Act II. One of these is sleep. In Act II Scene 2 Macbeth thinks he hears a voice saying 'Macbeth does murder sleep'. This suggests that his guilty conscience might not allow him to rest. His use of the verb 'murder' reminds us of his recent crime and implies that he killed his own capacity to sleep when he murdered King Duncan.

- Clear introduction to the paragraph
- Relevant quotation selected
- Analytical comment with effect
- Zooms in on key word

Now you try!

Finish this paragraph about another motif from Act II. Use one of the quotations from the list.

Another important motif in Act II is blood. In Act II Scene 2 Macbeth says ....

My progress Needs more work ☐ Getting there ☐ Sorted! ☐

9

PLOT AND STRUCTURE Act III Scenes 1-3

Three key things about Act III Scenes 1-3

1. Act III opens in **Macbeth's castle** as **Banquo** is **getting ready** to go **riding**.
2. We learn more about **Banquo**: he takes **no action** against Macbeth or to make the **witches' predictions** for his **descendants** come **true**.
3. The **motifs** of **darkness** and the **night** are explored.

What happens in Scene 1?

- Banquo is suspicious because Macbeth has everything that the witches promised.
- He thinks about the witches' momentous predictions for his family but then quickly dismisses these thoughts.
- Macbeth invites Banquo to attend his banquet and discovers that Banquo is going riding with his son, Fleance.
- Threatened by the witches' prediction that Banquo's offspring will be kings, Macbeth longs to make his own position more secure.
- Two murderers enter and Macbeth persuades them to kill Banquo and Fleance.

What happens in Scenes 2-3?

- **Scene 2:** Lady Macbeth is concerned because Macbeth has been spending too much time alone thinking.
- Macbeth tells his wife that he is worried about Banquo and Fleance but he does not tell her that he has arranged their murders.
- He implies that he is planning a crime and asks her to remain ignorant of his plans, but to admire his actions afterwards.
- **Scene 3:** Outside the castle, the two original murderers are joined by a third.
- When Banquo and Fleance appear on horseback, the men spring out and try to murder them.
- Banquo is killed but his son, Fleance, escapes.

Five key quotations

1. Banquo's suspicions about Macbeth: 'I fear/Thou played'st most foully for't' (III.1.2–3)
2. Macbeth's concerns about Banquo: 'For Banquo's issue have I fil'd my mind;/For them, the gracious Duncan have I murder'd' (III.1.66–7)
3. Macbeth's troubled mind: 'O, full of scorpions is my mind, dear wife!' (III.2.37)
4. The Macbeths' relationship: 'Be innocent of the knowledge, dearest chuck' (Macbeth to Lady Macbeth) (III.2.45)
5. The motif of darkness: 'Come, seeling night,/Scarf up the tender eye of pitiful day' (Macbeth) (III.2.46–7)

Note it!

Macbeth's appeal to **'seeling night'** in Act III Scene 2, associates him with darkness as he plans Banquo's murder. Darkness is connected to evil throughout the play. His words also link him to the evil of the witches who are **'midnight hags'**.

Exam focus

How can I write about Macbeth's relationships? AO1 AO2

You can use the first three scenes of Act III to focus on how these relationships change.

In Act III Scene 2, Shakespeare reveals a change in the relationship between Macbeth and Lady Macbeth when Macbeth does not tell her about his plan to murder Banquo and Fleance. Although he hints that he is planning a crime, he tells her to be 'innocent of the knowledge'. He also calls her 'chuck', which is an affectionate term but lacks the sense of power and equality of his earlier endearment 'partner of greatness'.

- Topic sentence makes overall point
- Relevant quotation selected
- Zooms in on key word
- Links to previous scene

Now you try!

Finish this paragraph about changes in Macbeth's relationship with Banquo at the beginning of Act III. Use one of the quotations from the list.

Macbeth's concerns about Banquo also change early in Act III. This is evident when ....

My progress Needs more work ☐ Getting there ☐ Sorted! ☐ 11

Three key things about Act III Scenes 4-6

1. **Scene 4** begins in the **banqueting hall of Macbeth's castle** as his **guests arrive** for a feast.

2. We learn more about **Macduff, the Thane of Fife**: he **refused to attend** the banquet and he is planning to go to **England** and gather support for an **army** to **depose Macbeth**.

3. The **themes** of the **supernatural** and **revenge** are developed.

What happens in Scene 4?

- Macbeth and Lady Macbeth host a banquet as king and queen.

- One of the murderers appears and tells Macbeth that Banquo is dead but that Fleance has escaped.

- Banquo's ghost appears to Macbeth at the feast and sits in Macbeth's chair. None of the other guests can see the ghost. Lady Macbeth makes excuses for her husband, telling them that he often has these fits.

- The ghost disappears and Macbeth regains his composure but then it appears again. Macbeth becomes even more agitated and Lady Macbeth has to ask their guests to leave.

- Macbeth believes that the ghost was seeking vengeance. He also feels threatened by Macduff's absence and decides to consult the witches again.

What happens in Scenes 5-6?

- **Scene 5:** Hecate, queen of the witches, is angry with the other three witches for not informing her about their dealings with Macbeth.

- She helps the witches to prepare a strong spell to deceive Macbeth.

- **Scene 6:** Lennox discusses recent events with a Lord. Lennox speaks with **irony**, suggesting that he no longer trusts Macbeth.

- The Lord reveals that King Duncan's son, Malcolm, has been welcomed in England by Edward, the English king, and that Macduff plans to join them.

Five key quotations

1. The theme of the supernatural: 'Thou canst not say I did it; never shake/Thy gory locks at me!' (Macbeth to Banquo's ghost) (III.4.50-1)
2. The theme of revenge: 'blood will have blood' (Macbeth) (III.4.122)
3. Lady Macbeth's view of the ghost: 'This is the very painting of your fear' (III.4.61)
4. The motif of blood: 'I am in blood/Stepp'd in so far that should I wade no more,/Returning were as tedious as go'er' (Macbeth) (III.4.136-8)
5. Lennox's use of irony: 'Did he not straight/In pious rage the two delinquents tear ...?' (III.6.11-12)

Note it!

The banquet scene marks a turning point for the Macbeths. At the start of the banquet they are at the height of their power but this is the last time that we see Lady Macbeth's self-control, and Macbeth is unable to keep calm at this important state occasion.

Exam focus

How can I write about the theme of the supernatural? (AO1) (AO2)

You can use Act III Scene 4 to write about how Shakespeare presents Banquo's ghost.

Here, Shakespeare raises questions about whether Banquo's ghost is supernatural or not. Lady Macbeth and the other guests can't see the ghost and Lady Macbeth refers to it as a 'painting' of Macbeth's fear. This implies that, in her opinion, the ghost is a work of his fevered imagination just like the dagger he saw prior to King Duncan's murder.	Clear topic sentence to introduce paragraph
	Development of previous point
	Relevant embedded quotation
	Link to a previous scene

Now you try!

Finish this paragraph about Macbeth's reaction to Banquo's ghost. Use one of the quotations from the list.

However, Macbeth believes that the ghost is real and he is terrified of it. This is evident when he tells it ....

PLOT AND STRUCTURE Act IV

Three key things about Act IV

1. **Act IV** begins with the **three witches** standing around their **cauldron**.
2. We are introduced to Macduff's wife, **Lady Macduff**, a **caring mother** who thinks her husband should not have abandoned his family.
3. Imagery is used to represent the state of Scotland: **suffering**, **sickness** and **enslavement**.

What happens in Scene 1?

- The three witches brew up a revolting potion.
- Macbeth arrives and commands them to answer him. They summon up apparitions who speak in riddles.
- An apparition of an armoured head warns Macbeth to **'beware Macduff'** and a bloody child tells him that **'none of woman born/Shall harm Macbeth'**.
- A child wearing a crown and carrying a branch says that Macbeth is safe until Birnam Wood comes to Dunsinane. Then a line of eight kings appears, followed by Banquo's ghost; this distresses Macbeth.
- The witches vanish and Lennox tells Macbeth that Macduff is in England. Macbeth decides to have Macduff's wife and children murdered.

What happens in Scenes 2-3?

- **Scene 2:** Lady Macduff and her son are at Macduff's castle. Ross tells Lady Macduff that her husband is in England.
- A messenger warns Lady Macduff she is in danger.
- Macbeth's hired murderers arrive and Lady Macduff and her children are killed.

- **Scene 3:** In England, Malcolm tests Macduff's loyalty by suggesting he, Malcolm, would be a worse king than Macbeth. He realises that Macduff is sincere when he laments the state of Scotland.
- A doctor speaks about King Edward of England's gifts of healing and prophecy.
- Ross informs Macduff that his family have been murdered. The distressed Macduff wants revenge.
- Malcolm, Macduff and the English army prepare to attack Macbeth's castle.

Five key quotations

1. Macbeth's evil: 'By the pricking of my thumbs,/Something wicked this way comes' (Second Witch) (IV.1.44–5)

2. Ross's view of the state of Scotland: 'know not what we fear,/But float upon a wild and violent sea' (IV.2.20–1)

3. Malcolm's view of Scotland's suffering: 'I think our country sinks beneath the yoke;/It weeps, it bleeds' (IV.3.39–40)

4. Macduff's distress: 'All my pretty ones?/Did you say all?' (IV.3.218–19)

5. Malcolm preparing to attack: 'Macbeth/Is ripe for shaking' (IV.3.240–1)

Note it!

Malcolm tests Macduff's loyalty because he wonders why Macbeth has not taken any action against Macduff. This is an example of dramatic irony because, unlike Malcolm, the audience knows that Macduff's family has already been killed. Their brutal murders also show us how low Macbeth has sunk.

Exam focus

How can I write about the state of Scotland? AO1 AO2

You can use Act IV to write about the imagery Shakespeare uses to describe Scotland:

> In Act IV Scene 3 Shakespeare uses negative imagery to represent the state of Scotland under Macbeth. For example, Malcolm claims that Scotland 'sinks beneath the yoke'. The verb 'sinks' indicates that Scotland is being oppressed and the noun 'yoke' suggests enslavement because a yoke is the wooden bar which was used to attach oxen to a plough.

- Clear topic sentence to introduce paragraph
- Quotation used to illustrate point
- Uses appropriate terminology
- Zooms in on key word

Now you try!

Finish this paragraph about how Shakespeare uses negative imagery for the state of Scotland. Use one of the quotations from the list.

Shakespeare also uses the image of a stormy sea to depict the state of Scotland under Macbeth's leadership. This is evident when ....

My progress Needs more work ☐ Getting there ☐ Sorted! ☐ 15

PLOT AND STRUCTURE Act V

Three key things about Act V

1. Act V sees the downfall and death of **Lady Macbeth** and **Macbeth**.
2. Malcolm, as **rightful king**, is restored to the throne.
3. The **themes** of **guilt**, **madness** and **revenge** are developed and concluded.

What happens in Scenes 1-2?

- **Scene 1:** A doctor and gentlewoman discuss Lady Macbeth's sleepwalking.
- While walking in her sleep, Lady Macbeth talks of murder and tries to wash imaginary blood from her hands.
- The doctor concludes that she needs divine help rather than medical attention.
- **Scene 2:** The rebel Scottish army prepares to attack Macbeth's castle.

What happens in Scenes 3-5?

- **Scene 3:** Macbeth hears that ten thousand soldiers are approaching but he remains confident due to the witches' predictions.
- The doctor tells Macbeth about his wife's illness.
- **Scene 4:** Malcolm's army cut down branches from Birnam Wood to use as camouflage.
- **Scene 5:** Macbeth hears his wife is dead and reflects on the meaninglessness of life.
- A messenger tells him that Birnam Wood is moving and Macbeth orders an attack.

What happens in Scenes 6-9?

- **Scene 6:** Malcolm's army throw down their branches and prepare to attack.
- **Scene 7:** Macbeth fights and kills young Siward.
- **Scene 8:** Macduff confronts Macbeth and reveals that he was born by caesarean section.
- Macduff fights and kills Macbeth and then cuts off his head.
- **Scene 9:** Malcolm is hailed as the new king of Scotland.

Five key quotations

1. Lady Macbeth's guilt: 'who would have thought the old man to have had so much blood in him?' (V.1.34–6)

2. Macbeth's despair: 'My way of life/Is fall'n into the sere, the yellow leaf' (V.3.22–3)

3. Macbeth's response to his wife's death: 'Out, out, brief candle,/Life's but a walking shadow, a poor player/That struts and frets his hour upon the stage' (V.5.22–4)

4. Macbeth's determination to fight: 'Why should I play the Roman fool and die/On mine own sword?' (V.8.1–2)

5. The theme of revenge: 'I have no words;/My voice is in my sword' (Macduff) (V.8.6–7)

Note it!

Note how this act is structured to build tension. The focus shifts quickly from Lady Macbeth to the English army to Macbeth. Most of the scenes are short and there are plenty of exits, entrances and hand-to-hand combat.

Exam focus

How can I use Act V to write about Macbeth? AO1 AO2

You can use Act V to discuss how Shakespeare portrays Macbeth's feelings about life.

In Act V Scene 3, Shakespeare uses the image of a 'yellow leaf' to reveal Macbeth's feelings of despondency. Macbeth seems to believe that his best days are over. His use of the word 'sere' suggests that his life is withering rather than flourishing. Shakespeare's autumnal image might also imply that, like a yellow leaf on an autumn tree, Macbeth is likely to fall from his lofty position and then die.

- Clear topic sentence to introduce paragraph
- Analytical comment showing effect
- Development of analysis
- Ends with personal interpretation

Now you try!

Finish this paragraph to show how Macbeth's responds to his wife's death. Use one of the quotations from the list.

After Lady Macbeth dies, Macbeth believes that life is ....

PLOT AND STRUCTURE Form and structure

Three key things about form and structure

1. The play is a **tragedy** which deals with the **downfall** of the **protagonist, Macbeth**.
2. We see his **rise** in the **first half** of the play and his **fall** in the **second**.
3. The play is in **five separate acts**, but we do not know if Shakespeare wrote it in this way.

What makes this play a tragedy?

- Tragedy is a form of classical drama associated with the Ancient Greeks and Romans.
- In classical tragedies the protagonist's fatal flaw results in his downfall; Macbeth's flaw is his ambition.
- Most of the action takes place at Macbeth's castle, which gives unity of place, and there is no **subplot**, which keeps our attention on the tragic hero, Macbeth.

How does the play's structure portray Macbeth's rise and fall?

- Act I is about Macbeth plotting to overthrow King Duncan and Act II sees him acting against King Duncan by killing him.
- Act III is a turning point where Macbeth is king but Fleance's escape from the murderers and Banquo's ghost distress him.
- From Act IV onwards other characters start to plot to overthrow Macbeth and Act V sees them fighting against him. Finally Macduff kills him.

How does Shakespeare use foreshadowing in the play?

- The first Thane of Cawdor was a traitor; this hints that Macbeth could become a traitor too.
- The witches' prediction that Macbeth will be king but Banquo's sons will be kings suggests that Banquo and Macbeth could come into conflict.
- The witches' predictions in Act IV **foreshadow** Macbeth's downfall in Act V.

Five key quotations

1. Ross's view of the first Thane of Cawdor: 'that most disloyal traitor' (I.2.52)
2. The witches' prediction for Banquo: 'Thou shalt get kings, though thou be none' (Third Witch) (I.3.65)
3. The First Apparition's warning: 'beware Macduff,/Beware the Thane of Fife' (IV.1.70–1)
4. Macbeth's downfall foreshadowed: 'I bear a charmed life which must not yield/To one of woman born' (V.8.12–13)
5. Macduff reveals how he was born: 'Despair thy charm, … Macduff was from his mother's womb/Untimely ripp'd' (V.8.13–16)

Note it!

Note that Macbeth and his wife pivot around the two-part structure of the play. Early on, Macbeth is troubled by his conscience while Lady Macbeth takes control of planning King Duncan's murder. By Act V these positions have reversed as her conscience is troubled while Macbeth has almost forgotten how to fear.

Exam focus

How can I write about structure? AO2

You can write about how Shakespeare uses foreshadowing in the play.

Shakespeare uses foreshadowing early in the play to give the audience a hint of what might happen later on.	Clear topic sentence introduces paragraph
One example of this is seen in Act I Scene 3, where the witches tell Macbeth he will become the Thane of Cawdor.	Develops previous point
Their prediction clearly foreshadows the moment soon afterwards when Duncan makes Macbeth Thane of Cawdor but it also hints that	Analytical comment
Macbeth might become a 'most disloyal traitor' just like the first owner of this title.	Embedded quotation with interpretation

Now you try!

Finish this paragraph about foreshadowing. Use one of the quotations from the list.

When Macbeth hears the apparitions' predictions in Act IV, he feels confident of success but they foreshadow his downfall. This is evident when ....

1. Look at this ideas map for Act IV. Is there anything else you could add?

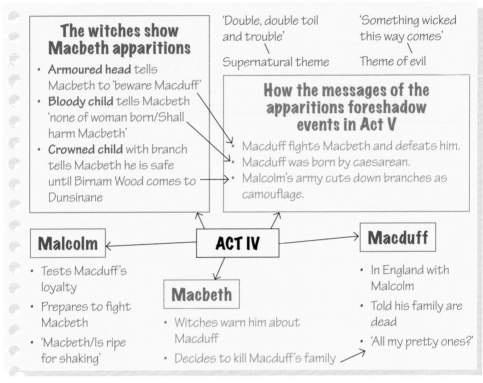

2. Create your own ideas map for one of the other acts.

Quick quiz

Answer these quick questions about plot and structure.

1. What is the weather like in the opening scene when the witches first appear?
2. Who tells Duncan that Macbeth decapitated the rebel Macdonald?
3. How does the first Thane of Cawdor die?
4. What do the witches predict for Banquo's descendants?
5. Who does King Duncan name as his successor?
6. What vision does Macbeth see just before he kills King Duncan?
7. Who discovers King Duncan's body?

8. Which men does Macbeth kill because he claims that they murdered Duncan?

9. Why do Malcolm and Donaldbain leave Macbeth's castle?

10. What is the name of Banquo's son who escapes from the murderers?

11. Where does Banquo's ghost sit at the banquet?

12. Who is the queen of the witches?

13. Why does a messenger visit Lady Macduff and her son shortly before they are murdered?

14. Who tells Macduff that his family have been murdered?

15. Which two characters watch Lady Macbeth sleepwalking?

16. Why does it look like Birnam Wood is moving in Act V?

17. Who does Macbeth fight and kill before he fights Macduff?

18. Who is hailed as king at the end of the play?

19. What is Macbeth's fatal flaw?

20. Which scene in Act III marks the turning point between Macbeth's rise and fall?

Power paragraphs

Write **a paragraph** in response to **each of these questions**. For each, try to **use one quotation** you have learned.

1. In what ways does Shakespeare contrast Macbeth and Banquo in Act I?

2. Why does Shakespeare include the discussion between Ross and the Old Man in Act II Scene 4?

Exam practice

Re-read Act V Scene 8, from line 1 'Why should I play the Roman fool' to line 17 'Accursed be that tongue that tells me so' where Macduff confronts Macbeth.

Why is this moment significant in the play as a whole? Write **two paragraphs** explaining your ideas.

You could comment on:

- the way that Macduff addresses Macbeth and what this reveals
- how confident Macbeth appears to be during this scene.

Five key things about Jacobean life and society

1. **Jacobean society** refers to **King James I's rule (1603–25)**.
2. Many people in Jacobean society went to **church** and schools reinforced **Christian teaching**.
3. **Women's role** in society was **limited** at this time.
4. **Poor** people **struggled** to survive, while the **rich** lived **lavishly**.
5. There were frequent **political conflicts**, **uprisings** and **plots** against the **king**.

How did the roles of men and women differ in Jacobean society?

- Education was mainly for boys, while girls stayed at home to learn domestic skills; very few girls were taught to read and write.
- Most married women looked after the children while their husbands went out to work.
- Masculinity was usually associated with strength and courage and femininity with nurturing and caring for children.

How could Christian teachings have influenced Macbeth?

- There are a number of Christian references in the play: Macbeth is associated with Hell and the Devil while King Duncan is **'sainted'**.
- In a Bible story about the Garden of Eden, Eve encourages Adam to eat forbidden fruit. Lady Macbeth persuades Macbeth to murder King Duncan in a similar way.
- Macbeth betrays Duncan for personal gain, just as Judas betrayed Jesus.

How could beliefs about witches have influenced Macbeth?

- King James was interested in witchcraft and wrote a book about it called *Daemonologie*, so Shakespeare could have included the witches to please him.
- Witches were commonly believed to have powers to conjure up apparitions and to vanish, as they do in the play.

Three key quotations

1. Lady Macbeth reverses gender roles: 'put/This night's great business into my dispatch' (Lady Macbeth, planning Duncan's murder) (I.5.66–7)

2. The witches' ability to vanish: 'what seem'd corporal,/Melted, as breath into the wind' (Macbeth, on the witches) (I.3.79–80)

3. The witches' power to summon spirits: 'raise such artificial sprites' (Hecate, about apparitions) (III.5.27)

Note it!

In Act I the Captain vividly describes the battle scene as **'another Golgotha'**. As Golgotha was the place where Christians believe Jesus died on the cross, the audience would have associated these words with pain and death.

Exam focus

How do I link context to the play? (AO3)

You can write about how far Shakespeare's presentation of women matches Jacobean expectations.

While Lady Macduff seems to represent the traditional Jacobean wife, Shakespeare's presentation of Lady Macbeth challenges traditional views about women. — Clear topic sentence establishes point

This is evident in Act I Scene 6 when she tells Macbeth to put the plans for King Duncan's murder into her 'dispatch'. — Supports point with evidence from the text

This behaviour might have seemed unusual to the Jacobean audience who could have expected her to follow her husband's lead. — Link to historical context

Now you try!

Finish this paragraph about how far Shakespeare's presentation of the witches reflects Jacobean beliefs. Use one of the quotations from the list.

In Jacobean times many people believed that witches could vanish into thin air. This power is seen in the play when ....

SETTING AND CONTEXT Succession and order

Five key things about succession and order

1. In Shakespeare's time there was **uncertainty** about the **royal succession**.
2. **Elizabeth I** died without children and was **reluctant** to **name** a **successor**.
3. The play **opens** with a **battle**, suggesting a **society in conflict**.
4. **James I** believed in the **divine right of kings** – that the **king's power** came from **God**.
5. Shakespeare uses **images** from the **natural world** to show how the rightful **succession** and the **Great Chain of Being** has been **disrupted**.

Why was the succession an important issue at the time?

- Since Henry VIII broke away from the Roman Catholic Church in the 1530s there had been many rebellions and conflicting claims on the throne.
- Elizabeth I didn't name James I as her successor until she was dying.
- James faced two plots to seize his throne in 1603 and an attempt to blow up Parliament in 1605 (the Gunpowder Plot).

How does Shakespeare use ideas about succession in the play?

- When King Duncan names Malcolm as his successor, Macbeth views Malcolm as an obstacle in his path.
- After the King's death, Macduff calls his murder **'sacrilegious'** and refers to Duncan's body as **'The Lord's anointed temple'** to reinforce the idea of the divine right of kings.
- King Edward of England is portrayed as being close to God as it is claimed he has the gifts of healing and prophecy.
- When Macbeth dies, Malcolm becomes king, restoring the rightful monarchy.

How does Shakespeare portray ideas about order in the play?

- When King Duncan dies, the Great Chain of Being, which Jacobeans believed was God's ordering of the universe, breaks down and Scotland suffers as a result.
- At Macbeth's banquet, his guests sit according to their ranks.

Three key quotations

1. The true line of succession: 'The son of Duncan,/From whom this tyrant holds the due of birth' (Lord, on Malcom) (III.6.24–5)

2. The idea that God supports the king: 'Macbeth/Is ripe for shaking, and the powers above/Put on their instruments' (Malcolm, about attacking Macbeth) (IV.3.240–2)

3. The rightful heir: 'To dew the sovereign flower and drown the weeds' (Lennox, about supporting Malcolm) (V.2.30)

Note it!

Macbeth and Malcolm have their coronations at Scone. Kings of Scotland were traditionally crowned at Scone Palace on a throne made of a block of stone. The real King Macbeth was crowned there in the eleventh century.

Exam focus

How can I write about order and succession? AO1 AO3

You can write about how Shakespeare implies that Malcolm is the rightful king.

> Clear topic sentence to introduce paragraph

Shakespeare uses natural imagery to represent Malcolm and Macbeth in Act V Scene 2, when Lennox speaks about the need to 'dew the sovereign flower and drown the weeds'. He compares Malcolm, the rightful heir, to a garden flower which they should take care of and Macbeth, who has taken his place, to an unwanted weed, suggesting that Macbeth has planted himself unlawfully on the throne.

> Supports point with relevant quotation

> Explanation of quotation

> Analysis and interpretation of quotation

Now you try!

Finish this paragraph about the idea that God supports the rightful king. Use one of the quotations from the list.

Malcolm and his followers want to remove Macbeth from power and restore the rightful monarchy. This is evident when Malcolm claims that ....

My progress Needs more work ☐ Getting there ☐ Sorted! ☐

SETTING AND CONTEXT Settings

Five key things about settings in the play

1. The play **begins** in **stormy weather** as a **brutal battle** rages between King Duncan's army and his enemies.
2. Much of the **action** takes place in **Macbeth's castle** in **Inverness**.
3. We visit **Macduff's castle once**, when his **family** are **murdered** there.
4. **Malcolm and Macduff** go to **England** to get help from the English king.
5. The witches imply **Macbeth** will **not** be **defeated** until **Birnam Wood moves**.

How do the settings in Act I Scenes 1-3 establish the mood of the play?

- The thunder and lightning create a sense of foreboding.
- The Captain's description of a bloody battle conjures up images of violent conflict.
- The witches' reference to **'filthy air'** suggests an unhealthy environment.

How is Macbeth's castle depicted in the play?

- Malcolm and Banquo describe Macbeth's castle as a pleasant place when they arrive there in Act I Scene 6.
- The Porter refers to the castle door as a **'hell-gate'** on the morning after Duncan's murder.
- The castle is the scene of the ferocious last battle during which Macbeth is attacked, defeated and killed.

What is the significance of Birnam Wood?

- The witches suggest that Macbeth is safe until Birnam Wood moves.
- Macbeth draws false confidence from the fact that trees cannot **'Unfix'** their roots.
- When Malcolm's army cut down branches as camouflage, the wood appears to move and the witches' prophecy is fulfilled.

How does Shakespeare portray England?

- England is portrayed as a safe country ruled by a religious king, Edward, who has the gift of prophecy and miraculously heals his subjects.
- England is used to contrast with Scotland which is depicted as bleeding and suffering under Macbeth's tyrannical leadership.

Quick quiz

Answer these quick questions about setting and context.

1. Why would King James I have enjoyed the supernatural scenes in the play?
2. What was the traditional role of a Jacobean wife?
3. How does Lady Macbeth resemble Eve in the Old Testament story about the Garden of Eden?
4. How did the guests at Macbeth's banquet know where to sit?
5. What was the divine right of kings?
6. What makes King Edward of England seem holy?
7. Where were Scottish kings crowned?
8. What impression do King Duncan and Banquo get of Macbeth's castle when they arrive there in Act I Scene 6?
9. Which is the only scene set at Macduff's castle?
10. How does Shakespeare describe Scotland's suffering under Macbeth's leadership?

Power paragraphs

Choose one key **setting** related to the play. Write **two paragraphs** explaining how Shakespeare makes use of this setting in relation to either a) theme or b) character.

CHARACTERS Macbeth in Acts I and II

Five key things about Macbeth in Acts I and II

1. Macbeth is **associated** with the **forces of darkness** through the **witches**.
2. He is **initially** shown as **brave** and **loyal to King Duncan**.
3. His loyalty is juxtaposed with his overarching **ambition**.
4. He seems **reluctant** to **kill the king** but is **persuaded by his wife** to do so.
5. His **guilty conscience** is suggested by the **dagger** he sees prior to killing Duncan.

What do we learn about Macbeth in Acts I and II?

- Macbeth is a Scottish lord who lives at Dunsinane with his wife, Lady Macbeth.
- The Captain reveals that Macbeth is a brave warrior who helped to defeat a rebellion against King Duncan.
- Macbeth is fascinated by the witches' predictions, which act as a driving force for his ambition.
- Lady Macbeth fears that Macbeth is **'too full o'th'milk of human kindness'** to kill Duncan.
- We learn that Lady Macbeth has a strong influence over Macbeth.
- Macbeth is prepared to commit murder in order to become king.

How does Macbeth's character develop?

- After his meeting with the witches, Macbeth is determined to become king. (Act I Scene 3)
- He believes that he needs to remove all the obstacles in his path to the throne, e.g. he decides to **'o'erleap'** Malcolm, Duncan's successor. (Act I Scene 4)
- After listening to his conscience, he decides not to murder King Duncan but Lady Macbeth persuades him to go ahead. (Act I Scene 7)
- He is distressed after the murder and feels he will never sleep peacefully again but he composes himself and pretends to be outraged when the body is discovered. (Act II Scenes 2 and 3)
- He changes from King Duncan's supporter to his murderer. (Act II Scene 2)

Five key quotations

1. Macbeth's bravery: 'O valiant cousin, worthy gentleman' (Duncan, I.2.24)
2. Fear of his murderous thoughts: 'why do I yield to that suggestion,/Whose horrid image doth unfix my hair' (I.3.133–4)
3. Wrestling with his conscience: 'should against his murderer shut the door,/ Not bear the knife myself' (I.7.15–16)
4. The theme of ambition: 'no spur/To prick the sides of my intent, but only/ Vaulting ambition' (I.7.25–7)
5. On Duncan's murder: 'I'll go no more./ I am afraid to think what I have done' (II.2.53–4)

Note it!

At the beginning of the play, Macbeth is described using positive **adjectives** such as **'valiant'** and **'worthy'**. However, his bravery in battle is also linked to verbs of violence such as **'carv'd'** and **'unseam'd'**. These suggest that Macbeth has a ruthless and brutal streak.

Exam focus

How can I write about Macbeth at the beginning of the play?

You can use Acts I and II to focus on how Macbeth fears his own murderous thoughts.

Shakespeare shows us Macbeth wrestling with his conscience in Act I Scene 3 when the 'suggestion' of murdering Duncan first enters his mind. Macbeth refers to this idea as a 'horrid image'. The adjective 'horrid' implies that he finds the thought shocking. When he asks 'why do I yield', the word 'yield' implies that he is giving in to murderous thoughts. In his inner battle between good and evil, the voice that asks 'why' represents his conscience.

| Clear topic sentence introduces paragraph |
| Uses appropriate terminology for analysis |
| Analysis of quotation |
| Ends with personal interpretation |

Now you try!

Finish this paragraph about Macbeth's reaction to Duncan's murder. Use one of the quotations from the list.

Macbeth's conscience is also apparent when he refuses to return to the scene of ....

Five key things about Macbeth in Acts III–V

1. Macbeth seems to **descend into evil** as he plans the murders of Banquo, Fleance and Macduff's family.
2. His **guilty conscience** troubles him in Act III when he sees **Banquo's ghost**.
3. He **seeks out the witches** in Act IV.
4. He shows **little emotion** when he hears about his **wife's illness** and responds to her death by **claiming that life is meaningless**.
5. His **castle is attacked** and he is **killed by Macduff**.

What do we learn about Macbeth in Acts III–V?

- Macbeth is the king of Scotland in Acts III, IV and most of Act V.
- In Act III Scene 2, Lady Macbeth tells Macbeth that he is spending too much time alone, thinking.
- Lady Macbeth suggests that Banquo's ghost is just a **'painting'** of his fear.
- Noblemen, who once supported Macbeth, turn against him.
- Malcolm observes that Scotland is suffering under Macbeth and plans to attack him.

How does Macbeth develop in Acts III–V?

- Macbeth feels threatened by the witches' prediction that Banquo's sons will be kings, so he hires murderers to kill Banquo and Fleance. (Act III Scene 3)
- He starts to keep his wife **'innocent'** of his plans for further murders. (Act III Scene 2)
- He seems terrified of Banquo's ghost in Act III, but by Act V he feels little fear. (Act III Scene 4 and Act V Scene 5)
- The witches' predictions give him confidence but he decides to secure his position by murdering Macduff's family. (Act IV Scene 1)
- After his wife's death, he feels that life is meaningless but he refuses to surrender and fights to the last. (Act V Scene 5)

Five key quotations

1. Macbeth's attitude to Banquo: 'Our fears in Banquo/Stick deep' (III.1.50–1)

2. On Banquo's ghost: 'Let the earth hide thee!/Thy bones are marrowless, thy blood is cold' (III.4.93–4)

3. On the things he has lost: 'that which should accompany old age,/As honour, love, obedience, troops of friends,/I must not look to have' (V.3.24–6)

4. On his determination to fight: 'They have tied me to a stake; I cannot fly,/ But bear-like I must fight the course' (V.7.1–2)

5. On his reluctance to fight Macduff: 'my soul is too much charg'd/With blood of thine already' (V.8.5–6)

Note it!

Note how Shakespeare uses language related to the underworld to describe Macbeth in the second half of the play. He is referred to as a **'devil'** and a **'hell-hound'**.

Exam focus

How can I write about Macbeth at the end of the play?

You can comment on whether the audience might feel sympathy for Macbeth in Act V.

> Some people might sympathise with Macbeth in Act V Scene 3 when he realises that he won't ever enjoy 'honour, love' or 'friends' again. Ironically, he was once honoured by Duncan, loved by his wife, and friends with Banquo, but his ambition resulted in the deaths of all these people. Perhaps his greatest loss is the loss of his wife and some of the audience might feel sympathy for Macbeth when he hears about her death.

Clear topic sentence to introduce paragraph
Development of previous point
Personal interpretation
Returns to key words from question

Now you try!

Finish this paragraph about Macbeth's determination to fight. Use one of the quotations from the list.

The audience might also sympathise with Macbeth in Act V when he says ....

Five key things about Lady Macbeth

1. Lady Macbeth has a **close relationship** with her **husband**.
2. She seems to be as **ambitious** as Macbeth.
3. Her **appeal** to **dark 'spirits'** associates her with the **witches** and their **evil**.
4. She has a **strong influence** over **Macbeth** early in the play but later she becomes **isolated** as he stops confiding in her.
5. Her **guilt** catches up with her in Act V when she **sleepwalks** and then **dies**.

What do we learn about Lady Macbeth?

- She is married to Macbeth and becomes queen in Act III.
- She is determined that Macbeth will be king, and persuades him to murder King Duncan.
- She plays the role of the perfect hostess to the king in a false display of welcome.
- She makes the arrangements for Duncan's murder and covers up the crime afterwards.
- When she sleepwalks in Act V, the doctor says she needs help from a priest rather than from him.

How does Lady Macbeth develop?

- After she reads about the predictions in Macbeth's letter, Lady Macbeth is determined that Macbeth will become king. (Act I Scene 5)
- She calls on spirits of darkness to remove her feminine qualities and manipulates Macbeth emotionally to murder King Duncan. (Act I Scene 5)
- She criticises Macbeth for his distress over killing Duncan and for his terror of Banquo's ghost. (Act II Scene 2 and Act III Scene 4)
- In Acts I–III she seems to feel little guilt, but by Act V her conscience catches up with her and she sleepwalks. (Act V Scene 1)
- It seems that her guilt drives her to suicide. (Act V Scene 5)

Five key quotations

1. Calling on evil spirits: 'Come, you spirits/That tend on mortal thoughts, unsex me here' (I.5.39–40)

2. On being prepared to kill her child: 'I would, while it was smiling in my face,/Have ... dash'd the brains out' (I.7.56–8)

3. Clearing her conscience of Duncan's murder: 'A little water clears us of this deed' (II.2.70)

4. On murdering Duncan: 'Had he not resembled/My father as He slept, I had done't' (II.2.12–13)

5. Her guilt: 'all the perfumes of Arabia will not sweeten this little hand' (V.1.44–5)

Note it!

Lady Macbeth appears to be connected to the witches when she calls on spirits of evil to fill her with cruelty. Malcolm calls her a **'fiend-like queen'**, reinforcing this idea.

Exam focus

How can I write about Lady Macbeth? (AO1)

You can focus on Acts I and II to show Lady Macbeth's attitude to her femininity.

In Act I Scene 5, Lady Macbeth appears to reject her femininity when she calls on spirits to 'unsex' her. This	Clear opening point
rejection is reinforced in Act I Scene 7 when she claims she would be prepared to dash her feeding child's 'brains out'.	Development of opening point
Lady Macbeth seems to associate femininity with weakness and masculinity with courage and strength.	Interpretation of text
The same belief is indicated when she manipulates Macbeth into murder by questioning his masculinity.	Further development of idea

Now you try!

Finish this paragraph about Lady Macbeth's guilt. Use one of the quotations from the list.

Lady Macbeth's feelings about having bloody hands, which symbolise guilt, change as the play progresses. In Act II, she ....
....

Five key things about Banquo

1. Banquo is presented as **brave** and **loyal** to **King Duncan**.
2. He seems **ambitious** when he asks for a **personal prediction** from the witches.
3. He **suspects** that there may be **evil motives** behind the witches' prophecies.
4. He becomes **suspicious** of **Macbeth** after King Duncan's murder.
5. **Macbeth** arranges to have him **killed** but he **appears as a ghost** and as one of the **witches' apparitions**.

What do we learn about Banquo?

- Banquo is a nobleman and a soldier in King Duncan's army.
- King Duncan calls him **'Noble'** after he fights alongside Macbeth against Duncan's enemies.
- The witches predict that Banquo's descendants will be kings. He reflects on this promise and hopes it will come true.
- He refuses to swear loyalty to Macbeth as king and has suspicions about how Macbeth gained the crown.
- Macbeth cannot forget Banquo after his death as he is haunted by his ghost.

What is Banquo's function in the play?

- Banquo provides a contrast with Macbeth in his reaction to the witches' prophecies: he takes no action to make the witches' promises for his family come true. (Act I Scene 3)
- The witches' predictions about his descendants set the scene for conflict because Macbeth sees him as a threat. (Act III Scene 3)
- Banquo's murder and Fleance's escape add tension and drama to the play. (Act III Scene 3)
- His appearance as a ghost at Macbeth's banquet and as an apparition allow Shakespeare to develop the **themes** of guilt and the supernatural. (Act III Scene 4 and Act IV Scene 1)

Five key quotations

1. His suspicion of the witches' predictions: 'oftentimes, to win us to our harm,/The instruments of darkness tell us truths' (I.3.122–3)

2. Banquo's character: 'He hath a wisdom that doth guide his valour' (Macbeth) (III.1.54)

3. On Macbeth becoming king: 'I fear/Thou played'st most foully for't' (III.I 2–3)

4. His tentative hope for the witches' predictions: 'May they not be my oracles as well/And set me up in hope? But hush, no more' (III.1.9–10)

5. Macbeth on Banquo as a threat: 'They hail'd him father to a line of kings./Upon my head they plac'd a fruitless crown' (III.I.61–2)

Note it!

Shakespeare's patron, King James I of England, was a descendant of the real Banquo so Shakespeare would have wanted to portray his ancestor in a good light. However, in Shakespeare's source for the play, *Holinshed's Chronicles*, Banquo helped Macbeth to murder King Duncan.

Exam focus

How can I write about Banquo?

You can focus on how Shakespeare presents Banquo's reaction to the witches' prophecies.

> Shakespeare suggests that Banquo is suspicious of the witches in Act I Scene 3 when he warns Macbeth that 'oftentimes, to win us to our harm,/The instruments of darkness tell us truths'. By associating the witches with 'darkness', Banquo implies that they are evil and the word 'harm' suggests that their promises might be dangerous. He seems to be telling Macbeth that even though the witches' predictions may come true, they should not be trusted.

Clear opening using relevant quotation

Analytical comment with effect

Zooms in on a word

Interpretation of quotation

Now you try!

Finish this paragraph about Macbeth's view of Banquo. Use one of the quotations from the list.

Once Macbeth becomes king, Banquo becomes a threat to him. This is evident when ....

Three key things about Macduff

1. Macduff is the **Thane of Fife**, a married nobleman.
2. He **abandons** his **family** when he goes to **England** and his **wife and children** are **murdered**. He **vows** to **avenge** their **deaths**.
3. He does not attend Macbeth's coronation or banquet and he **kills Macbeth** in Act V.

What is Macduff's function in the play?

- When Macduff does not attend Macbeth's coronation or banquet, it seems that he mistrusts Macbeth. (Act III Scene 4)
- When the witches warn Macbeth about Macduff, he becomes an obstacle in Macbeth's path which places his family in danger. (Act IV Scene 1 and Act IV Scene 2)
- Macduff was born by caesarean section so he fulfils the witches' prediction that Macbeth should fear someone who is not **'of woman born'**. (Act IV Scene 1)

Three key things about Lady Macduff

1. Lady Macduff is **Macduff's wife**, and the mother of his children.
2. She only **appears once** in the play, just before **she** and **her children** are **murdered**.
3. She is portrayed as **defenceless** and **vulnerable**.

What is Lady Macduff's function in the play?

- Her character contrasts with Lady Macbeth's as she is presented as a caring mother. (Act IV Scene 2)
- Her murder arouses the audience's pity and reveals Macbeth's evil. (Act IV Scene 3)
- Her death is part of the motivation for Malcolm, Macduff and the English army to attack Macbeth's castle. (Act IV Scene 3)

Five key quotations

1. Lady Macduff on Macduff: 'Wisdom? To leave his wife, to leave his babes' (IV.2.6)

2. Lady Macduff on protecting children, and foreshadowing their fate: 'for the poor wren,/The most diminutive of birds, will fight,/Her young ones in her nest, against the owl' (IV.2.9–11)

3. Macduff about his family's murder: 'What, all my pretty chickens and their dam/At one fell swoop?' (IV.3.220–1)

4. Malcolm on Macduff's positive qualities: 'Macduff, this noble passion, ... thy good truth and honour' (IV.3.114–17)

5. Macduff revealing how he was born: 'Macduff was from his mother's womb/Untimely ripp'd' (V.8.15–16)

Note it!

When Macduff discovers Duncan's dead body, he struggles to find words to express his grief and exclaims **'Tongue nor heart cannot conceive, nor name thee'**. In contrast, Macbeth uses exaggerated, flowery phrases such as **'His silver skin lac'd with his golden blood'** in order to appear grief-stricken.

Exam focus

How can I write about Lady Macduff? AO1 AO2

You can comment on how Shakespeare portrays Lady Macduff as a caring mother.

Shakespeare portrays Lady Macduff as a caring mother in Act IV Scene 2 when she speaks about a 'poor wren' fighting to protect her nest from an owl. Lady Macduff's words suggest parents should protect their children and imply criticism of Macduff for leaving them. However, a wren is a small bird and an owl would tear it apart, so her words also foreshadow the fact that she and her family will soon be murdered.

- Clear topic sentence containing well-chosen quotation
- Analysis of quotation
- Development of analysis
- Interpretation

Now you try!

Finish this paragraph about Macduff. Use one of the quotations from the list.

Macduff is very distressed by the brutal murders of his family. This is evident when ....

My progress Needs more work ☐ Getting there ☐ Sorted! ☐

Three key things about King Duncan

1. **Duncan** is the **king of Scotland** at the beginning of the play.
2. He is presented as **virtuous, generous** and **trusting**.
3. He is **murdered** in his sleep by **Macbeth**.

What is King Duncan's function in the play?

- Duncan's kingship contrasts with Macbeth's: King Macbeth is suspicious and tyrannous but King Duncan appears to be fair and saintly. (Act I Scene 7)
- The build-up to his murder and the discovery of his body are tense and dramatic. (Act II Scenes 1–3)
- After his death, Scotland becomes chaotic, and the tension builds further as his son, Malcolm, prepares to attack Macbeth's castle in order to avenge Duncan's death. (Act IV Scene 3)

Three key things about Malcolm

1. **Malcolm** is **King Duncan's eldest son**, and Duncan names him as **his successor**.
2. He **escapes to England** after his father's murder as he **fears he may be murdered** too.
3. He does not seem to be as trusting as his father and he **tests Macduff's loyalty**.

What is Malcolm's function in the play?

- When Malcolm is named as Duncan's successor, Macbeth's thoughts turn to murder. (Act I Scene 5)
- Malcolm's army is presented as a force of goodness fighting against Macbeth's evil. (Act IV Scene 3)
- When Malcolm is hailed as king, Shakespeare implies that the rightful succession has been restored. (Act V Scene 9)

Five key quotations

1. Duncan on the first Thane of Cawdor: 'He was a gentleman on whom I built/An absolute trust' (I.4.13–14)

2. Macbeth on Duncan: 'this Duncan/Hath borne his faculties so meek, hath been/So clear in his great office' (I.7.16–18)

3. Duncan on Malcolm: 'We will establish our estate upon/Our eldest, Malcolm' (1.4.37–8)

4. Malcolm after Duncan's murder: 'This murderous shaft that's shot/Hath not yet lighted, and our safest way/Is to avoid the aim' (II.3.137–9)

5. Malcolm's honesty: 'delight/No less in truth than life' (IV.3.129–30)

Note it!

Note how Shakespeare uses Duncan's positive qualities as a generous and virtuous king to contrast with Macbeth's tyrannical leadership. After his death, Duncan is remembered as a **'sainted king'** while Macbeth is referred to as a **'dead butcher'**.

Exam focus

How can I write about King Duncan?

You can write about how Shakespeare presents King Duncan as trusting.

Although King Duncan has many virtues, his trusting nature could be perceived as a weakness. In Act I Scene 4 Duncan states that he placed 'An absolute trust' in the first Thane of Cawdor. However, Cawdor was not worthy of this trust and betrayed him. Ironically, Duncan awards Cawdor's title to Macbeth and once again this trust is misplaced because Macbeth murders him and takes his throne.	Clear opening point with personal interpretation
	Relevant embedded quotation
	Development
	Analytical comment

Now you try!

Finish this paragraph about Malcolm after Duncan's murder. Use one of the quotations from the list.

Malcolm *does not seem to be as trusting as his father. This is evident when he decides to flee from* ....

CHARACTERS The witches

Five key things about the witches

1. The witches are associated with the **themes** of the **supernatural** and **appearance and reality**.
2. They speak in **riddles** and often use **rhyming couplets**.
3. They seem **evil** and appear to have some **knowledge of the future**.
4. They have some **magical powers** such as the ability to **vanish** into thin air and to **summon** apparitions.
5. They are presented as **deceptive** and **dangerous**.

What do we learn about the witches?

- The witches seem to be supernatural beings who are visible to both Macbeth and Banquo. Their queen is Hecate.
- They predict that Macbeth will become Thane of Cawdor then king and tell Banquo that his sons will be kings.
- Their gender is uncertain: Banquo says that they should be women but they have beards.
- Macbeth is fascinated by them, but Banquo fears they have evil intentions.
- In Act IV they summon up apparitions who tell Macbeth to beware of Macduff, of a man not born of a woman and of Birnam Wood moving.

What is the witches' function in the play?

- They add mystery, drama and a supernatural element to the play. (Act I Scenes 1 and 3 and Act IV Scene 1)
- They reflect the evil in the world. (Act IV Scene 1)
- Their predictions act as a motivation for Macbeth's ambition. (Act I Scene 3)
- Ultimately, their predictions prompt Macbeth to kill Duncan, Banquo and Macduff's family. (Act II Scene 2, Act III Scene 1 and Act IV Scene 1)
- Their riddles give Macbeth a false confidence but in the end he realises that their words were designed to deceive him. (Act V Scene 8)

Five key quotations

1. First Witch, on meeting again: 'When shall we three meet again?/In thunder, lightning, or in rain?' (I.1.1–2)
2. The witches' appearance: 'you should be women,/And yet your beards forbid me to interpret/That you are so' (Banquo) (I.43–5)
3. Their ability to vanish: 'Melted, as breath into the wind. Would they had stay'd' (Macbeth) (I.3.80)
4. Mixing their potion: 'Double, double toil and trouble;/Fire burn, and cauldron bubble' (IV.1.10–11)
5. Macbeth on the witches: 'And be these juggling fiends no more believ'd/ That palter with us in a double sense' (V.8.19–20)

Note it!

Note that Hecate, queen of the witches, is not always included in productions of *Macbeth*. This is because some people believe that Shakespeare did not write her lines and that they were added at a later date.

Exam focus

How can I write about the witches? AO2

You can focus on how Shakespeare presents the witches' language.

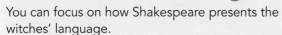

Shakespeare uses the witches' language to make them sound mysterious.	Topic sentence makes overall point
They use contradictory phrases such as 'Fair is foul', suggesting that nothing is what it seems.	Quotation used to illustrate point
Macbeth realises this in Act V Scene 8 when he claims that the witches 'palter' in a 'double sense', implying that they trick people by using ambiguous language.	Analysis of quotation
He also calls them 'juggling fiends' which suggests that he believes that they play with words for evil purposes.	Development of analysis

Now you try!

Finish this paragraph about the witches' language. Use one of the quotations from the list.

Shakespeare also makes the witches sound mysterious when they speak in rhyming couplets. When they are mixing their potion, they chant ....

1. Look at this ideas map about Macbeth. Is there anything else you could add?

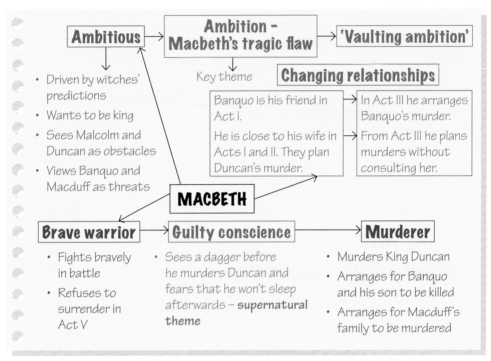

2. Create your own ideas map for one of the other characters.

Quick quiz

Answer these quick questions about characters.

1. Who has 'a wisdom that doth guide his valour'?

2. What positive characteristic does Macbeth show in the Act I battle against King Duncan's enemies?

3. Who persuades Macbeth to kill King Duncan after he has decided not to carry out the crime?

4. Who is the Thane of Fife?

5. Which character fears that Macbeth 'played'st most foully' to become king?

6. Why won't Macbeth return the daggers after he has killed King Duncan?

7. Why do some directors leave Hecate out of their productions of the play?
8. How does Lady Macduff feel about her husband going to England?
9. Why does Macbeth decide to have Banquo and his son murdered?
10. How does Lady Macbeth die?
11. How many scenes does Lady Macduff appear in?
12. Who is the king of Scotland in Acts III, IV and most of Act V?
13. Which characters often speak in riddles and **rhyming couplets**?
14. Why does Lady Macbeth claim that she could not murder the sleeping King Duncan?
15. What do the witches do with the 'Eye of newt, and toe of frog'?
16. Which two important events does Macduff miss because he mistrusts Macbeth?
17. What does Lady Macbeth try to wash from her hands as she sleepwalks?
18. How was Macduff born?
19. Which scenes do the witches appear in?
20. Who does Malcolm refer to as a 'dead butcher'?

Power paragraphs

Write **a paragraph** in response to **each of these questions**. For each, try to **use one quotation** you have learned from this section.

1. Why is Lady Macduff's murder a significant event in the play?
2. Why do you think Shakespeare includes the witches brewing up a potion in Act IV Scene 1?

Exam practice

Re-read Lady Macbeth's speech in Act II Scene 2, from 'That which hath made them drunk' (line 1) to 'I had done't' (line 13).

What do we learn about Lady Macbeth from these lines? Write **two paragraphs** explaining your ideas. You could comment on:

- the language she uses
- the nature of her thoughts.

THEMES Ambition

Five key things about the theme of ambition

1. **Ambition** is central to the play as it is the **fatal flaw** that leads to Macbeth's downfall and death.
2. The **witches** and **Lady Macbeth** are able to **influence Macbeth** because of his **ambition**.
3. **Ambition** makes **Macbeth tyrannous** and **murderous**.
4. **Ambition** is also explored through **Lady Macbeth**.
5. **Banquo** has **ambitions** but he **takes no action** to fulfil them.

How does Shakespeare present Macbeth's ambition?

- When King Duncan names Malcolm as his successor, Macbeth sees Malcolm as an obstacle in his path.
- Macbeth admits that ambition is his only reason for killing Duncan.
- Macbeth's ambition is more powerful than his conscience.
- His ambition is not satisfied once he is king as he wants to make sure that his position is secure.
- He tries to destroy those who threaten his power.

How do other characters help develop the theme?

- Lady Macbeth is ambitious for her husband and fears he lacks the cruelty necessary to succeed. Shakespeare shows how she persuades Macbeth to murder King Duncan.
- When Macbeth has doubts about killing King Duncan, Lady Macbeth convinces him to go ahead with the murder plan by questioning his masculinity.
- After the witches tell Macbeth he will be king, Banquo asks them to speak to him and thinks carefully about their prediction that his descendants will become kings.
- Unlike Macbeth, Banquo is suspicious of the witches and, although he has ambitions, he does not act on them.

Five key quotations

1. Lady Macbeth on Macbeth: 'Thou wouldst be great,/Art not without ambition, but without/The illness should attend it' (I.5.17–19)

2. Macbeth on Malcolm being named heir: 'that is a step/On which I must fall down, or else o'erleap' (1.4.48–9)

3. Macbeth considering murdering King Duncan: 'no spur/To prick the sides of my intent, but only/Vaulting ambition' (I.7.25–7)

4. Macbeth feeling threatened by Banquo: 'To be thus is nothing,/But to be safely thus' (III.1.49–50)

5. Banquo asking the witches to predict his future: 'If you can look into the seeds of time/And say which grain will grow and which will not,/Speak then to me' (I.3.56–8)

Note it!

Shakespeare presents Macbeth as a tragic hero. In classical tragedies, the **protagonist** suffers and dies because of a fatal flaw in his character. Macbeth's ambition causes him to kill the King, setting off a chain of events that leads to his downfall.

Exam focus

How can I write about Macbeth's ambition? AO1 AO2

You can write about how Macbeth reacts to Malcolm being named Duncan's heir.

Shakespeare reveals Macbeth's ambition in Act I Scene 4 when he describes Malcolm as 'a step/On which I must fall down, or else o'erleap'. The words 'step' and 'o'erleap' imply that he wants to climb ahead of Malcolm in the order of succession. His determination is indicated by his use of the strong modal verb 'must'. Macbeth claims that Malcolm is 'in [his] way' which suggests that he views him as an obstacle.	Clear opening using relevant quotation
	Analytical comment showing effect
	Zooms in on word
	Development of previous points

Now you try!

Finish this paragraph about ambition. Use one of the quotations from the list.

Shakespeare also reveals Macbeth's ambition when he claims his only reason for murdering King Duncan is ....

My progress Needs more work ☐ Getting there ☐ Sorted! ☐

Five key things about the themes of betrayal and revenge

1. **Betrayal and revenge** are closely **linked** since those who are betrayed seek revenge.
2. The **Thane of Cawdor** betrays **King Duncan**, so he is **executed** by him.
3. **Macbeth murders King Duncan**, so his son, **Malcolm**, seeks revenge.
4. **Macbeth** betrays **Banquo**, by arranging his **murder**. He believes **Banquo's ghost haunts** him in revenge.
5. **Macbeth** betrays **Macduff** by hiring **murderers** to kill **his family**, and Macduff **kills** Macbeth to avenge them.

How does Shakespeare develop the theme of betrayal?

- The first Thane of Cawdor betrays King Duncan, which **foreshadows** the fact that Macbeth, the second Thane of Cawdor, will also betray him.
- When Macbeth betrays King Duncan by murdering him, he sets in motion the chain of events which together form the **tragedy**.
- Nobles like Macduff and Lennox join Malcolm, which highlights Macbeth's increasing isolation.
- Shakespeare also suggests that Macbeth's cruel leadership betrays Scotland because the country then **'weeps'** and **'bleeds'**.

How does Shakespeare develop the theme of revenge?

- Banquo's ghost haunts Macbeth, which is a form of revenge and also adds drama and tension to the play.
- When Fleance escapes from the murderers, Shakespeare leaves us wondering if he will return to avenge his father's death or take the throne.
- Malcolm attacks Macbeth's castle and claims the throne in the belief that his revenge will heal the wounded Scotland.
- Macduff avenges his family's murders by killing Macbeth, which fulfils the witches' prophecies.

Five key quotations

1. King Duncan on the first Thane of Cawdor: 'No more that Thane of Cawdor shall deceive/Our bosom interest. Go pronounce his present death' (I.2.63–4)

2. Macbeth, after seeing Banquo's ghost: 'They say: blood will have blood' (III.4.122)

3. Menteith on Malcolm and Macduff: 'Revenges burn in them' (V.2.3)

4. Malcolm on healing Scotland: 'Let's make us med'cines of our/To cure this deadly grief' (IV.3.216–17)

5. Macduff to Macbeth: 'If thou be'st slain, and with no stroke of mine,/My wife and children's ghosts will haunt me still' (V.7.16–17)

Note it!

Note that the theme of betrayal can be linked to the theme of appearance and reality. For example, when Macbeth and Lady Macbeth welcome King Duncan to their castle, appearing to be kind hosts, they deliberately hide their intention to betray the king's trust by murdering him.

Exam focus

How can I write about revenge?

You can write about the imagery Shakespeare uses to represent revenge.

Shakespeare associates revenge with an image of fire in Act V Scene 2 when Menteith claims that 'Revenges burn' in Malcolm and Macduff. The word 'burn' suggests that their desire for revenge may be fuelled by their anger at the crimes committed against them. In Shakespeare's time fire was associated with purification, so this image could also imply that their revenge might rid Scotland of Macbeth's evil.

Clear opening using relevant quotation

Analysis of quotation

Link to historical context

Interpretation of quotation

Now you try!

Finish this paragraph about revenge. Use one of the quotations from the list.

Shakespeare also suggests that Malcolm's revenge could heal Scotland. This is evident when Malcolm suggests that ....

Five key things about the theme of the supernatural

1. The **appearance** of the **three witches** in Act I Scene 1 **establishes** the **supernatural** theme.
2. The supernatural elements in *Macbeth* bring **magic, drama and mystery** to the play.
3. **Lady Macbeth** is associated with **dark forces** when she calls on spirits to 'unsex' her and fill her with **cruelty**.
4. **Macbeth's visions** of the **dagger** and **Banquo's ghost** appear to be supernatural but they could be created by Macbeth's **guilty conscience**.
5. The supernatural **predictions** of the witches both **hide** and **reveal** the **truth**.

How is the supernatural presented through the witches?

- The witches are the first characters we see. Their appearance in thunder and lightning creates a disturbing atmosphere and sets the scene for the action that follows.
- The witches represent evil in the world and own familiars (evil spirits in the form of animals) such as **'Greymalkin'** (a cat) and **'Paddock'** (a toad).
- The witches' predictions act as a driving force for Macbeth's ambition and the plot itself.
- The witches never tell Macbeth to commit murder, so their supernatural power is not directly responsible for his actions.
- Their predictions do, however, foreshadow events in Act V.

Are Macbeth's visions supernatural or psychological?

- Shakespeare raises questions about witchcraft and psychology in the play.
- Whereas Banquo sees the witches with Macbeth, only Macbeth can see the dagger and Banquo's ghost.
- Macbeth himself suggests that the dagger might be just a sign of his troubled mind and Lady Macbeth says the ghost is a **'painting'** of his fear.
- Macbeth seems to be particularly affected by the supernatural: he is fascinated by the witches' words.

Five key quotations

1. First Witch on her familiar: **'I come, Greymalkin'** (I.1.9)
2. First Witch on creating a storm: **'Though his bark cannot be lost,/Yet it shall be tempest-toss'd'** (I.3.23–4)
3. Macbeth on the dagger he sees: **'A dagger of the mind, a false creation,/Proceeding from the heat-oppressed brain?'** (II.1.38–9)
4. Macbeth on Banquo's ghost: **'Take any shape but that, and my firm nerves/Shall never tremble'** (III.4.102–3)
5. Macbeth on the witches: **'Infected be the air whereon they ride,/And damn'd all those that trust them'** (IV.1.137–8)

Note it!

Modern directors present the supernatural elements of the play according to their interpretations of the text. If, for example, they decide that Banquo's ghost will appear, the audience is more likely to believe that it is supernatural rather than imaginary.

Exam focus

How do I write about the supernatural? AO1

You can write about how Shakespeare makes the supernatural seem evil.

> Shakespeare implies that the witches' supernatural powers are evil in Act I Scene 3 when the First Witch claims that a sailor's boat will be 'tempest-toss'd'. This suggests that the witches deliberately create storms at sea. The First Witch also appears to regret the fact that they can only shake the ship rather than sinking it. Furthermore, her image of a rough sea might reflect the problems that their evil will bring to Macbeth.

Clear opening using relevant quotation

Interpretation of quotation

Development of previous point

Ends with personal interpretation

Now you try!

Finish this paragraph about the witches' evil. Use one of the quotations from the list.

The witches are also presented as evil when Macbeth calls the air on which they ride ......

Five key things about the theme of fate and free will

1. Shakespeare leaves us to decide if Macbeth's **rise and fall** was **fated** to happen **or** if it **resulted** from his **own choices**.

2. The **witches** never tell Macbeth to kill anybody, so it could be argued that their **predictions** are **morally neutral**.

3. In **Act I** the **witches plan** to meet **Macbeth**; in **Act IV he chooses** to visit them.

4. **Macbeth chooses not** to **listen** to **his conscience**, or to **Banquo's warning** that the witches' words may be dangerous.

5. **Macbeth allows himself** to be **influenced** by the **witches** and his **wife**.

How far does Macbeth determine his own fate?

- Macbeth could have waited to see if he became king without taking any action.
- Macbeth has plenty of reasons not to kill King Duncan, but he goes ahead with the murder because of his ambition.
- Banquo is Macbeth's friend, but Macbeth decides to kill him and Fleance to secure the throne.
- An apparition tells Macbeth to be wary of Macduff, but it does not tell him to murder Macduff's wife and children.
- Macbeth fears he is destined to die when Macduff finally confronts him, but he chooses to fight rather than surrender.

How far do other characters influence Macbeth's decisions?

- The witches' suggestion that Macbeth will become king sows the seeds for murder.
- Lady Macbeth encourages Macbeth to kill Duncan and takes control of the arrangements for the murder.

- Lady Macbeth persuades Macbeth to change his mind after he decides not to kill Duncan.
- The witches' promises for Banquo and their warning about Macduff prompt Macbeth to plan more murders.

Five key quotations

1. Macbeth, after he is made Thane of Cawdor: 'This supernatural soliciting/Cannot be ill, cannot be good' (I.3.129–30)

2. Macbeth on the predictions: 'If chance will have me king, why chance may crown me' (I.3.142)

3. Macbeth on choosing not to kill Duncan: 'We will proceed no further in this business' (I.7.31)

4. Macbeth plotting murder: 'Fleance, his son …/Whose absence is no less material to me/Than his father's, must embrace the fate/Of that dark hour' (III.1.137–40)

5. Macbeth vowing to fight on: 'Though Birnam Wood be come to Dunsinane/ And thou oppos'd being of no woman born,/Yet I will try the last' (V.8.30–3)

Note it!

The word 'weird' in 'weird sisters' means fate or destiny. This title might connect the three witches to the three fates in Greek mythology who were believed to have power over humans and their lives.

Exam focus

How does Shakespeare portray the theme of fate and free will? AO1

You can write about the choices that Macbeth makes during the play.

Macbeth does not wait for 'chance' to 'crown' him king; he murders King Duncan to make the witches' prediction come true. Although his wife convinces him to commit the crime after he had decided to 'proceed no further', he chooses to go through with it, recognising his only motive for killing Duncan is 'Vaulting ambition'. Therefore, Duncan's murder appears to be an act of free will.

| Clear topic sentence to introduce paragraph |
| Introduces argument |
| Develops argument |
| Sums up using question key words |

Now you try!

Finish this paragraph about another of Macbeth's choices. Use one of the quotations from the list.

Macbeth also seems to make a clear decision to murder Banquo's son, Fleance. This is evident when Macbeth tells ....

THEMES Appearance and reality

Five key things about the theme of appearance and reality

1. Shakespeare presents the **theme** of **appearance and reality** through **ambiguous language** such as the **witches' riddles**.
2. The appearance of certain settings, like Birnam Wood, is misleading.
3. Some **characters put on acts** to **deceive** others.
4. The audience can observe the **difference** between appearance and reality through listening to asides, soliloquies and **private conversations**.
5. **Macbeth** has **visions** that **other characters cannot see**.

How does Shakespeare develop the theme?

- While Duncan describes Macbeth's castle as a pleasant place, the audience know it is the setting for his murder.
- When Macbeth and his wife pretend to welcome the king to their castle, King Duncan trusts them.
- The witches' riddles make Macbeth believe that he has a **'charmed life'**, but their words foreshadow his downfall and death.
- Malcolm pretends to be a bad leader to test Macduff, which suggests that he is a suspicious character.
- Birnam Wood appears to move, even though trees cannot uproot themselves, suggesting that the other predictions will also come true.

What clues does Shakespeare give the audience?

- Shakespeare uses soliloquies and asides to show the audience his characters' true thoughts.
- He also allows the audience to overhear private conversations such as Macbeth and Lady Macbeth's discussion about murdering Duncan.
- Shakespeare uses dramatic irony, e.g. when Malcolm suggests that Macbeth has done nothing to harm Macduff but the audience knows that Macduff's family has already been killed.
- Macbeth is the only one who can see Banquo's ghost and the dagger, which suggests they may be not real.

Five key quotations

1. The witches' ambiguous language: 'Lesser than Macbeth, and greater' (I.3.63)

2. Macbeth on disguising his true intentions: 'Stars, hide your fires,/Let not light see my black and deep desires' (I.5.50–1)

3. Lady Macbeth on a deadly disguise: 'look like th'innocent flower/But be the serpent under't' (I.5.64–5)

4. Macbeth on deception: 'False face must hide what the false heart doth know' (I.7.82)

5. Birnam Wood starts to move: 'I look'd toward Birnam and anon methought/The wood began to move' (Messenger) (V.5.33–4)

Note it!

When Lennox speaks about Macbeth in Act III his words seem to hide his true thoughts. He says nothing against Macbeth but when he asks **'Did he not straight/In pious rage the two delinquents tear ...?'**, his ironic tone suggests that Macbeth could have killed the grooms for more evil reasons.

Exam focus

How can I write about appearance and reality? AO1 AO2

You can write about the witches' ambiguous language.

Shakespeare presents the theme of appearance and reality through the witches' ambiguous language because their riddles often conceal the truth. For example in Act I Scene 3, the words 'Lesser than Macbeth, and greater' are difficult to interpret because 'Lesser' and 'greater' (like 'fair' and 'foul') are opposites. In fact, the negative term 'lesser' masks the fact that Banquo will be murdered.

- Clear topic sentence to introduce paragraph
- Supports point with evidence from the text
- Analysis of quotation
- Interpretation of quotation

Now you try!

Finish this paragraph about appearance and reality. Use one of the quotations from the list.

Shakespeare also shows characters deliberately hiding their true thoughts or intentions. This is seen when Lady Macbeth ....

My progress Needs more work ☐ Getting there ☐ Sorted! ☐

THEMES Guilt and madness

Five key things about the theme of guilt and madness

1. **Guilt** and **madness** are closely **connected**: one seems to lead to the other.
2. Shakespeare uses the motifs of **sleeplessness** and **blood** to represent **guilt**.
3. Initially, **Lady Macbeth** shows **no guilt** about killing King Duncan but **later** her **guilty conscience catches up with her**.
4. **Macbeth** feels **guilty** after **King Duncan's murder** but **later** he feels **less remorse**.
5. **Macbeth's visions** of **Banquo's ghost** and the **dagger** might **indicate** his **guilty conscience**.

How does Shakespeare present Macbeth's guilt and madness?

- Macbeth is not afraid to kill in battle but he is distressed after killing King Duncan and claims **'every noise appals me'**.
- He thinks he hears a voice saying **'Sleep no more'**. This is probably his guilty conscience.
- His guilty conscience may also produce his visions of the dagger and Banquo's ghost. He almost reveals his guilt when he sees the ghost.
- Macbeth shows signs of paranoia when he sees Banquo as a threat.
- In Act V, Macbeth shows little guilt but he is reluctant to fight Macduff because the murders of Macduff's family are on his conscience.

How does Shakespeare present Lady Macbeth's guilt and madness?

- Initially Lady Macbeth seems to feel no guilt about killing Duncan and is critical when Macbeth feels distressed.
- In Act V her guilt sees her sleepwalking and carrying a light because she fears the darkness.
- She probably commits suicide because of her troubled conscience.
- When Lady Macbeth is in control of her emotions she speaks in blank verse, but as she becomes mentally disorientated, Shakespeare uses broken up phrases of prose to illustrate her state of mind.

Five key quotations

1. Lady Macbeth, after Duncan's murder: 'These deeds must not be thought/After these ways; so, it will make us mad' (II.2.36–7)
2. Macbeth's mental disturbance: 'Methought I heard a voice cry, "Sleep no more"' (II.2.38)
3. Macbeth to Banquo's ghost: 'Thou canst not say I did it; never shake/Thy gory locks at me!' (III.4.50–1)
4. Lady Macbeth's agitation, while sleepwalking: 'Out, damned spot! Out, I say!' (V.1.31)
5. Macbeth's loss of guilt: 'my slaughterous thoughts/Cannot once start me' (V.5.14–15)

Note it!

Shakespeare uses images of blood and water to illustrate this **theme**. After Duncan's murder, Macbeth believes **'great Neptune's ocean'** won't wash the blood from his hands, while Lady Macbeth claims **'A little water'** will clean them. However, when she sleepwalks in Act V she is trying to wash imaginary blood from her hands.

Exam focus

How can I write about guilt and madness? AO2

You can write about Lady Macbeth's language in Act V Scene 1.

Shakespeare indicates Lady Macbeth's guilt and mental disturbance in Act V Scene 1 by the way she talks when she is sleepwalking. She speaks in snatches of prose, such as 'Out, damned spot! Out, I say!' Her repetition of 'out' and the exclamation marks suggest the strength of her agitated feelings. We also notice that she no longer uses blank verse as she did in Acts I–III which suggests a loss of control.

Clear topic sentence to introduce paragraph

Supports point with evidence from the text

Analysis and interpretation of quotation

Development of point

Now you try!

Finish this paragraph about Macbeth. Use one of the quotations from the list.

Shakespeare reveals that Macbeth's mind is disturbed when ....

1. Look at this ideas map on the **theme** of betrayal and revenge. Is there anything else you could add?

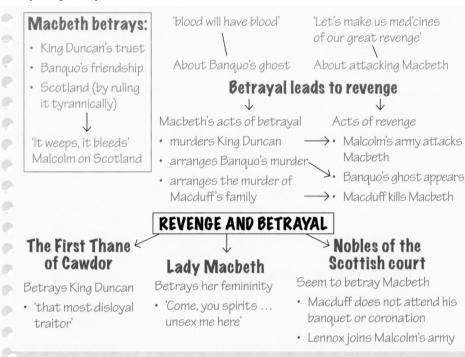

Macbeth betrays:
- King Duncan's trust
- Banquo's friendship
- Scotland (by ruling it tyrannically)

↓

'It weeps, it bleeds'
Malcolm on Scotland

'blood will have blood'

\

About Banquo's ghost

'Let's make us med'cines of our great revenge'

\

About attacking Macbeth

Betrayal leads to revenge

↓   ↓

Macbeth's acts of betrayal   Acts of revenge

- murders King Duncan ⟶ • Malcolm's army attacks Macbeth
- arranges Banquo's murder ⟶ • Banquo's ghost appears
- arranges the murder of Macduff's family ⟶ • Macduff kills Macbeth

REVENGE AND BETRAYAL

The First Thane of Cawdor

↓

Lady Macbeth

Nobles of the Scottish court

Betrays King Duncan
- 'that most disloyal traitor'

Betrays her femininity
- 'Come, you spirits ... unsex me here'

Seem to betray Macbeth
- Macduff does not attend his banquet or coronation
- Lennox joins Malcolm's army

2. Create your own ideas map for one of the other themes.

Quick quiz

Answer these quick questions about themes.

1. Which characters establish the supernatural theme in Act I?
2. The witches' predictions can be described as morally neutral. What does this mean?
3. What makes Macbeth conclude that Malcolm is an obstacle in his path?
4. Which of the witches' promises, does Banquo hope will come true?
5. What does Macbeth believe is his only reason for killing King Duncan?
6. How are the themes of betrayal and appearance and reality linked?
7. Which character is executed in Act I for betraying King Duncan's trust?

8. What does the word 'weird' mean in the title 'weird sisters'?

9. Who convinces Macbeth to kill King Duncan after he decides not to go ahead with the murder plan?

10. Why does Macbeth's second meeting with the witches seem like an act of free will, while his first visit does not?

11. What crime does Macduff want to avenge when he fights Macbeth?

12. How does Macbeth feel straight after King Duncan's murder?

13. What does Macbeth mean when he says that Malcolm's army is 'forc'd with those that should be ours'?

14. What does Lady Macbeth always carry with her when she sleepwalks?

15. How does Macbeth react to Banquo's ghost at the banquet?

16. Which two of the witches' predictions does Macduff fulfil in Act V Scene 8?

17. Why do some people think that Banquo's ghost is not a supernatural being?

18. Name two **motifs**, other than sleeplessness, that Shakespeare uses to represent guilt.

19. When does Macbeth see Banquo's ghost for a second time?

20. Which word is missing from the quotation 'look like th'innocent flower,/But be the … under't'?

Power paragraphs

Write **a paragraph** in response to **each of these questions**. For each, try to **use one quotation** you have learned from this section.

1. How does the first appearance of the witches establish the theme of the supernatural?

2. How does Shakespeare use the motif of sleeplessness to symbolise guilt?

Exam practice

Re-read Banquo's **soliloquy** in Act III Scene I, lines 1–10.

What do we learn about the theme of ambition from these lines? Write **two paragraphs** explaining your ideas. You could comment on:

• Banquo's fears about Macbeth's success

• his hopes regarding the witches' prediction for his family.

My progress Needs more work ☐ Getting there ☐ Sorted! ☐

LANGUAGE Imagery and symbolism

Five key things about Shakespeare's use of imagery and symbolism

1. Shakespeare uses imagery to **paint vivid pictures** in the audience's minds.
2. He uses personification to illustrate the **troubled state of Scotland** under Macbeth.
3. He uses simile and metaphor to illustrate **characters' hidden thoughts**.
4. Symbols **represent ideas and themes**, e.g. blood which represents guilt.
5. Motifs are used to emphasise their importance and draw attention to **key ideas**.

How does Shakespeare use imagery to illustrate the state of Scotland?

● Ross's image of a **'wild and violent sea'** implies that, under Macbeth, Scotland is turbulent and dangerous.
● Shakespeare uses personification to show that Scotland is suffering when Malcolm says that it **'weeps'** and **'bleeds'**.

How does Shakespeare use imagery to illustrate characters' thoughts?

● Banquo's simile: **'A heavy summons lies like lead upon me,/And yet I would not sleep'** suggests he feels weighed down by worries so he can't sleep.
● Macbeth's metaphor: **'We have scorch'd the snake, not kill'd it'** suggests that although Macbeth is king, he still feels threatened by Banquo.

How does Shakespeare use symbolism?

● Light and darkness symbolise good and evil, e.g. King Duncan says that **'nobleness like stars shall shine'**, while Macbeth appeals to **'seeling night'**.
● Motifs of blood and sleeplessness symbolise guilt, e.g. Lady Macbeth washes imaginary blood from her hands and Macbeth thinks a voice cries, **'Sleep no more'**.

Five key quotations

1. Simile: 'pity, like a naked new-born babe/Striding the blast, or heaven's cherubin … Shall blow the horrid deed in every eye' (Macbeth on murdering King Duncan) (I.7.21–4)

2. Metaphor: 'a giant's robe/Upon a dwarfish thief' (Angus on Macbeth stealing Duncan's throne) (V.2.21–2)

3. Personification: 'dark night strangles the travelling lamp' (Ross, suggesting it is unnaturally dark) (II.4.7)

4. Imagery: 'make thick my blood' (Lady Macbeth, asking for strength) (I.5.42)

5. Motif of blood: 'who would have thought the old man to have had so much blood in him?' (Lady Macbeth, sleepwalking) (V.1.34–6)

Note it!

Shakespeare uses images of birds and animals to describe Macduff's murdered family. Macduff refers to the family as **'my pretty chickens'** and Ross calls them **'murder'd deer'**. These images portray them as innocent and vulnerable, and present Macbeth's crime as unnatural.

Exam focus

How can I write about Shakespeare's use of imagery?

You can focus on Shakespeare's use of simile to illustrate Macbeth's betrayal.

Shakespeare uses a simile in Act I Scene 7 when Macbeth compares the pity that would arise from Duncan's murder to a 'naked new-born babe' and 'heaven's cherubin'.	Clear opening using relevant quotation
These images suggest Duncan's innocence.	Analysis of quotation
They also indicate Macbeth's fear that murdering the king could bring divine punishment, since cherubs often surround God in religious paintings.	Development of analysis
This reflects the Jacobean belief that killing the king was a crime against God.	Link to historical context

Now you try!

Finish this paragraph about how Macbeth betrays King Duncan. Use one of the quotations from the list.

Shakespeare uses a metaphor to suggest that it was wrong to steal Duncan's throne when in Act V ....
....

LANGUAGE Dramatic techniques

Five key things about Shakespeare's dramatic techniques

1. Shakespeare's **theatre** and **audience influenced** his **dramatic techniques**.
2. Soliloquies and asides reveal characters' **secret thoughts**.
3. **Spoken descriptions** give the audience **clues** about settings.
4. Dramatic irony allows the **audience** to **know more** than certain characters.
5. Some stage directions have **symbolic** meanings.

How did Shakespeare's theatre influence his dramatic techniques?

- Shakespeare's theatre had no scenery so some characters tell us where they are, e.g. King Duncan comments on Macbeth's pleasant castle.
- A Jacobean audience did not sit in silence. So including dramatic scenes helped to keep their attention.
- Sound effects such as an owl shrieking build tension and key props such as the daggers enhance the action.

Which techniques does Shakespeare use to reveal his characters' secret thoughts?

- Shakespeare uses soliloquies, e.g. when Macbeth wrestles with his conscience about murdering King Duncan. (Act I Scene 7)
- He also uses asides, e.g. when Macbeth concludes that Malcolm is an obstacle in his path. (Act I Scene 5)

What other dramatic techniques does Shakespeare use?

- Dramatic irony is used, e.g. when Malcolm wonders why Macbeth has not touched Macduff and the audience knows about Macduff's family.
- The porter creates a comic interlude between King Duncan's murder and its discovery. The porter speaks in **prose**, rather than the **blank verse** used by the nobles, to show his lower social status.
- Some of Shakespeare's stage directions are symbolic, e.g. the witches appear in thunder and lightning to symbolise their evil.

Five key quotations

1. Soliloquy: 'Hie thee hither,/That I may pour my spirits in thine ear' (Lady Macbeth, persuading Macbeth to kill Duncan) (I.5.24–5)

2. Aside: 'Glamis, and Thane of Cawdor:/The greatest is behind' (Macbeth on the witches' promises) (I.3.116)

3. Dramatic irony: 'Conduct me to mine host: we love him highly/And shall continue our graces towards him' (King Duncan on Macbeth before Macbeth kills him) (I.6.30–1)

4. Setting the scene: 'The west yet glimmers with some streaks of day' (First Murderer, waiting to attack Banquo) (III.3.5)

5. Reference to sounds: 'I heard the owl scream and the crickets cry' (Lady Macbeth, waiting for Macbeth to kill Duncan) (II.2.15)

Note it!

In Shakespeare's theatre a trap door on stage allowed characters or props to disappear. In Act IV Scene I, the stage directions state that the apparitions 'descend', probably through this trap door. This could also symbolise their descent into Hell.

Exam focus

How can I write about Shakespeare's dramatic techniques? AO2

You can focus on how Shakespeare uses dramatic techniques to set the scene.

> Shakespeare uses the First Murderer's atmospheric description in Act III Scene 3 to build tension before Banquo's murder. He describes the light fading as the sky 'glimmers with some streaks of day'. This could represent the last moments before Banquo's brutal murder. The fact that it is almost dark might also imply evil since Shakespeare often uses darkness to represent evil in 'Macbeth'.

- Clear topic sentence to introduce paragraph
- Development of previous point
- Interpretation of quotation
- Link to rest of the play

Now you try!

Finish this paragraph about how Shakespeare uses dramatic techniques to build tension. Use one of the quotations from the list.

Shakespeare also uses sound to build tension when his characters hear strange noises ....

My progress Needs more work ☐ Getting there ☐ Sorted! ☐

Five key things about the exam

1. You will have **one** question on *Macbeth* which will be based on a **passage** given to you on the exam paper.
2. It will focus on **Shakespeare's presentation** of an aspect of the play, such as a **character, relationship** or theme.
3. You will have about **45–50 minutes** to read and respond to the question.
4. The question is worth **30 marks**.
5. The question assesses **AOs 1, 2, 3, with an extra 4 marks for AO4**. Remember that **AO3** relates to '**context**'.

What will a question look like?

1. Starting with this extract, explore how Shakespeare presents Lady Macbeth as forceful.

Write about:

- how Shakespeare presents Lady Macbeth as forceful in this extract
- how Shakespeare presents Lady Macbeth as forceful in the play as a whole.

[30 marks] AO4 [4 marks]

You must refer to the given passage

You must explain the techniques Shakespeare uses

This is the area you must tackle

A reminder to begin with the given passage/ extract

A reminder to **also** write about the whole of the play

Do all questions look the same?

- Not all questions will begin this way. Some might contain **statements** you must argue for or against, e.g. '**Shakespeare's presentation of Lady Macduff enables the reader to feel sympathy for her.' Starting with this extract, explore how far you agree with this opinion.**
- Not all questions will be about a single character. Some might ask you about a **relationship** between two characters, e.g. between Macbeth and Lady Macbeth.

What do I need to do to get a good mark?

Use this grid to understand what your current level is and how to improve it:

	AO1 Read, understand, respond	**AO2** Analyse language, form, structure and effects	**AO3** Show understanding of contexts
High	• You make **precise references** to the **passage** and *Macbeth* **as a whole**. • Your argument is **well-structured**, with **quotations** fluently **embedded** in sentences. • You cover **both** the extract and the whole play.	• You **analyse** and **interpret** the methods Shakespeare uses **very effectively**. • You **explore thoughtfully** the effects of these on the reader. • You show **excellent use** of subject terminology.	• You make **detailed, relevant links** between specific elements of the play and social, historical contexts.
Mid	• You make a **range of references** to the passage and the play as a whole. • You respond in **a clear, logical way** with **relevant** quotations chosen.	• You **explain clearly** some of the methods Shakespeare uses, and **some effects** on the reader. • You use **mostly relevant** subject terminology.	• You show **clear evidence** of understanding context which is **linked** to the play in places.
Lower	• You make **some references** to the passage and play as a whole, but in rather a **patchy** way. • You make **some useful points** but evidence is **not always clear or relevant**.	• You make **occasional attempts** to explain Shakespeare's methods but these are a little **unclear**. • You show **some use** of subject terminology.	• You demonstrate **basic awareness** of context but **links** to the play are **undeveloped** and **not always relevant**.

AO4 You can also gain up to 4 marks for **AO4**, which assesses your use of spelling, punctuation and grammar. For top marks: use a **range** of vocabulary and sentence structures, adopt a **clear, purposeful and effective** writing style, and make sure your spelling and punctuation is **accurate**.

Read this exam-style character question

Read this extract from Act V Scene 5 of *Macbeth* and then answer the question that follows.

At this point in the play Malcolm's army are about to attack Macbeth's castle.

> **MACBETH**
> Hang out our banners on the outward walls;
> The cry is still, 'They come.' Our castle's strength
> Will laugh a siege to scorn; here let them lie
> Till famine and the ague eat them up.
> 5 Were they not forc'd with those that should be ours,
> We might have met them dareful, beard to beard,
> And beat them backward home.
> *A cry within of women.*
>   What is that noise?
>
> **SEYTON**
> It is the cry of women, my good lord.
>
> **MACBETH**
> I have almost forgot the taste of fears;
> 10 The time has been, my senses would have cool'd
> To hear a night-shriek and my fell hair
> Would at a dismal treatise rouse and stir
> As life were in't. I have supp'd full with horrors;
> Direness familiar to my slaughterous thoughts
> 15 Cannot once start me. Wherefore was that cry?

2. Starting with this moment in the play, explore how far Shakespeare presents Macbeth as being fearless.

Write about:

- how Shakespeare presents Macbeth as fearless in this scene
- how Shakespeare presents Macbeth as fearless in the play as a whole.

[30 marks] AO4 [4 marks]

NOW read this further character question

Read this extract from Act I Scene 4 and answer the question that follows.

At this point in the play the first Thane of Cawdor, who betrayed King Duncan's trust, has just been executed.

> **DUNCAN**
> There's no art
> To find the mind's construction in the face.
> He was a gentleman on whom I built
> An absolute trust.
> *Enter* Macbeth, Banquo, Ross *and* Angus
> O worthiest cousin,
> 15 The sin of my ingratitude even now
> Was heavy on me. Thou art so far before,
> That swiftest wing of recompense is slow
> To overtake thee. Would thou hadst less deserv'd
> That the proportion both of thanks and payment
> 20 Might have been mine. Only I have left to say,
> More is thy due than more than all can pay.
>
> **MACBETH**
> The service and loyalty I owe,
> In doing it, pays itself. Your highness' part
> Is to receive our duties, and our duties
> 25 Are to your throne and state, children and servants,
> Which do but what they should by doing everything
> Safe toward your love and honour.

3. 'Shakespeare's presentation of King Duncan suggests that he is too trusting of others.'

Starting with this extract, explore how far you agree with this statement.

Write about:

- how Shakespeare presents Duncan as trusting in this scene
- how Shakespeare presents Duncan as trusting in the play as a whole.

[30 marks] AO4 [4 marks]

EXAM PRACTICE Planning your character response

Five key stages to follow

1. **Read** the **question**; **highlight** key words.
2. **Read** the **passage** with the **key words** from the **question** in mind.
3. Quickly **generate ideas** for your response.
4. **Plan** for paragraphs.
5. **Write** your response; **check it** against your plan as you progress.

What do I focus on?

Highlight the **key words**:

> 2. Starting with this moment in the play, explore how far Shakespeare presents Macbeth as being fearless.
>
> Write about:
>
> - how Shakespeare presents Macbeth as fearless in this scene
> - how Shakespeare presents Macbeth as fearless in the play as a whole.
>
> **[30 marks] AO4 [4 marks]**

What do they tell you? Focus on both extract and whole text; explain what specific methods Shakespeare uses; stick to Macbeth's fearlessness as main topic.

How should I read the passage?

- Check for any immediate links to the question (e.g. Macbeth is confident in the strength of his defences).
- Look for any evidence/quotations you could highlight (e.g. **'almost forgot the taste of fears'**)

How do I get my ideas?

Note your ideas in a spider diagram or list them in a table:

The extract

Confidence in strength of castle: 'laugh a siege to scorn'

Macbeth seems to have lost his sense of fear?

Macbeth's fearlessness

The play as a whole

Confident in battle

Fearful: Duncan's murder & Banquo's ghost

The extract	The play as a whole
• Macbeth is confident that his defences will hold	• Macbeth is confident in battle – Act I
• Macbeth claims to feel little fear	• Macbeth shows fear earlier in the play, e.g. Banquo's ghost – Act III

HOW do I structure my ideas?

Make a **plan** for **paragraphs**.* Decide the order for your points:

- Paragraph 1: Go straight into your first point: *In this extract, Macbeth is preparing for battle – confident – personifies castle 'laugh a siege to scorn'. Earlier, in Act I, he was also portrayed as a confident warrior by the Captain.*
- Paragraph 2: *In this scene he is outnumbered and betrayed but still fearless. In Act I, when he was bravely fighting the Norwegians, the opposing forces seemed more equally matched as the outcome was 'Doubtful'*
- Paragraph 3: *Emotionally numb – 'forgot the taste of fears' – was fearful earlier, e.g. in Act III, when he sees Banquo's ghost*
- Paragraph 4: *He has become used to murder – 'supp'd full with horrors'*
- Paragraph 5: *The cry – builds tension – hair image link to 'doth unfix my hair' – previous fear lost*

HOW do I write effectively?

Write **clear**, **analytical** paragraphs and **embed** your evidence fluently, e.g.:

In the extract, Shakespeare shows us Macbeth preparing for battle. Macbeth adopts a commanding tone, suggesting that he does not fear his enemies. He seems confident that his 'castle's strength' can withstand their attack. Earlier in the play, he is equally confident in battle as the Captain calls him 'brave', but he shows fear after King Duncan's murder when 'every noise appals' him. It could be said that he can face up to fear as a soldier, but not as a king.

Overview point – extract

Key term

Quotations are embedded in the sentence

Link to rest of play

Summary point

Now you try!

Re-read Question 3 on page 65 and plan your response in the same way.

* The plan above and the sample answers have five paragraphs but you don't need to be limited to this if you have more points to include.

What does a Grade 5 answer look like?

Read the task again, then the sample answer below.

2. Starting with this moment in the play, explore how far Shakespeare presents Macbeth as being fearless.

Write about:

- how Shakespeare presents Macbeth as fearless in this scene
- how Shakespeare presents Macbeth as fearless in the play as a whole.

[30 marks] AO4 [4 marks]

In this passage Macbeth is confidently preparing for a battle against Malcolm's army. At the start of the extract he is giving out orders such as 'Hang out our banners' and this makes him sound in control of the situation. He also uses personification about his castle which he says will 'laugh a siege to scorn'. The word 'scorn' means mock so this shows that he thinks the strength of his castle will easily prevent Malcolm from attacking it.

AO1 Clear statement setting out viewpoint

AO2 Close reference to word use and what it means

Macbeth seems fearless because he isn't bothered that the other army have more soldiers than him. He says they are 'forc'd with those that should be ours'. This means that some of the men who used to support him have moved over to Malcolm's army. When we heard about Macbeth winning a battle in Act I Scene 2, the armies seemed equally matched, but this time he is facing a more difficult challenge. However, he doesn't seem frightened to take on the challenge.

AO1 Clear progression to next point but rather informal

AO2 Clear link made to elsewhere in the play

In this passage, Macbeth suggests that he has forgotten how to feel frightened. He says 'I have almost forgot the taste of fears'. This is different from other scenes in the play. Ghost scene being an example.

AO2 This doesn't add anything as there is no analysis

AO4 This is not a complete sentence

It seems as though Macbeth is not frightened because he has done too many evil things. This is seen when he says 'I have supp'd full with horrors' meaning that he has killed so many people that he has stopped worrying about it. I think he was a better person when he did feel some fear after killing Duncan and Banquo because this showed that he had a conscience.

Paragraph 4

Macbeth also hears a cry in this passage which could have frightened him. In Shakespeare's day they did not have much scenery, so noises like this were used to build up tension. When Macbeth hears the cry he remembers a time when a noise like that would have scared him. I think he may be remembering his fear after killing King Duncan when he says 'every noise appals me'. At that time he was more fearful and I think it was because he felt guilty but now he has lost his guilt so he has also lost his fear.

Paragraph 5

Check the skills

Re-read paragraphs four and five of this response and:

● Highlight other **points** made
● Circle any reference to **context**
● Underline any places where the student has made an **interpretation**

Now you try!

Look again at paragraph three ('*In this passage, Macbeth suggests that he has forgotten …*', etc.) and improve it by:

● Adding a **reference or quotation** to show Macbeth's fear of Banquo's ghost
● **Explaining** why Shakespeare uses the word 'taste' in the quotation 'I have almost forgot the taste of fears'
● Ending with a **summary point** about how Macbeth has changed
● Improving the overall **style** by making sure your sentences **flow**; using connectives to **link** ideas

What does a Grade 7+ answer look like?

Read the task again, then the sample answer below.

2. Starting with this moment in the play, explore how far Shakespeare presents Macbeth as being fearless.

Write about:

- how Shakespeare presents Macbeth as fearless in this scene
- how Shakespeare presents Macbeth as fearless in the play as a whole.

[30 marks] AO4 [4 marks]

In this passage, Shakespeare uses Macbeth's commanding tone to reflect his fearlessness in the face of an imminent attack. Before this extract, he was told that ten thousand men were approaching his castle, but he plans to confront them bravely. Macbeth signals his intention to fight by telling his soldiers to 'Hang out our banners' as banners were used to display the colours of opposing forces in battle. He also personifies his castle's strength as 'laughing a siege to scorn', suggesting confidence in the face of Malcolm's assault.

> **AO1** Clear statement sets out argument

> **AO2** Structural link made with evidence to earlier in play

> **AO3** Excellent knowledge of context linked to Shakespeare's viewpoint

Shakespeare implies that Macbeth has been forced to defend his position when he would rather launch an attack because his forces are outnumbered. Although Macbeth is an experienced soldier, Malcolm's army presents a greater threat than the Norwegian forces he faced in Act I because, in that instance, the two armies seemed closely matched. Yet he remains fearless and defiant.

> **AO1** Excellent summary sentence

> **AO4** Well-constructed sentence develops argument

In spite of these challenges, Macbeth claims to have almost forgotten 'the taste of fear'. His use of the word 'taste' suggests he has retained sensory memories of the physiological changes that accompany fear. These recollections may have arisen from earlier when Macbeth was fearful, for example, of Banquo's ghost. Here, Macbeth seemed to fear this 'horrible shadow' more than a living enemy since it could not be killed with a 'sword'. This could imply that he finds it easier to be brave when he faces physical conflict rather than psychological stress.

> **AO1** Fluent link to new aspect of argument

> **AO2** Carefully selected evidence and detailed analysis of language use and effect

> **AO1** Point is developed and interpreted

In this passage, Shakespeare also suggests that Macbeth feels little fear because he has 'supp'd full with horrors', suggesting that his unnatural deeds have numbed his natural responses. This might partly explain his display of bravery in this passage, but it could be argued that if Macbeth had allowed himself to feel more fear, he might not have ended up in such a dangerous situation since this fear might have prevented him from committing regicide.

Half way through this extract, there is a sudden cry. In Shakespeare's time, there was little scenery, so sound effects were used to build up tension. When Macbeth hears the cry he is not affected by it but tells Seyton that once such noises made his hair stand on end. These words remind us of the 'horrible imaginings' which he claimed 'unfix[ed]' his hair as he contemplated King Duncan's murder. It is possible that he killed his capacity to fear when he stopped listening to his conscience.

Paragraph 4

Paragraph 5

Check the skills

Re-read paragraphs four and five of this response and:

- Identify any particularly **fluent** or **well-expressed** ideas
- Find any further references to **context**
- Highlight any places where the student has shown **deeper insight** and offered **original** or particularly **thoughtful** ideas or made interesting **links**

Now you try!

Now, using the plan you made for Question 3 on page 67, write a full response. Here's a reminder of the question:

2. 'Shakespeare's presentation of King Duncan suggests that he is too trusting of others.'

   Starting with this extract, explore how far you agree with this statement.

   Write about:

   - how Shakespeare presents Duncan as trusting in this scene
   - how Shakespeare presents Duncan as trusting in the play as a whole.

   [30 marks] AO4 [4 marks]

- Try to match your answer to the High Level objectives on page 63.

71

Read this exam-style theme question

Read this extract from Act I Scene 5 of *Macbeth* and then answer the question that follows.

At this point in the play Lady Macbeth and Macbeth are plotting to kill King Duncan when he visits their castle.

LADY MACBETH

O never
60   Shall sun that morrow see.
     Your face, my thane, is as a book where men
     May read strange matters. To beguile the time,
     Look like the time, bear welcome in your eye,
     Your hand, your tongue; look like th'innocent flower,
65   But be the serpent under't. He that's coming
     Must be provided for, and you shall put
     This night's great business into my dispatch,
     Which shall to all our nights and days to come
     Give solely sovereign sway and masterdom.

MACBETH

70   We will speak further –

LADY MACBETH

Only look up clear;
     To alter favour ever is to fear.
     Leave all the rest to me.

---

4. Starting with this conversation, explore how Shakespeare presents appearance and reality in *Macbeth*.

   Write about:

   ● how Shakespeare presents appearance and reality in this extract

   ● how Shakespeare presents appearance and reality in the play as a whole.

   [30 marks] AO4 [4 marks]

Now read this further theme question

Read this extract from Act III Scene 4 of *Macbeth* and then answer the question that follows.

At this point in the play Macbeth believes he can see Banquo's ghost at the royal banquet.

> **LADY MACBETH**
> O proper stuff!
> This is the very painting of your fear;
> This is the air-drawn dagger which you said
> Led you to Duncan. O, these flaws and starts,
> Impostors to true fear, would well become
> 65 A woman's story at a winter's fire
> Authoriz'd by her grandam. Shame itself!
> Why do you make such faces? When all's done
> You look but on a stool.
> **MACBETH**
> Prithee, see there! Behold, look, ho! How say you?
> 70 [*To* Ghost] Why, what care I? If thou canst nod, speak too.
> If charnel-houses and our graves must send
> Those that we bury back, our monuments
> Shall be the maws of kites.   [*Exit* Ghost of Banquo]
> **LADY MACBETH**
> What, quite unmann'd in folly.
> **MACBETH**
> As I stand here, I saw him.

5. Starting with this conversation, explore how Shakespeare presents the supernatural in *Macbeth*.

   Write about:

   ● how Shakespeare presents the supernatural in this conversation

   ● how Shakespeare presents the supernatural in the play as a whole.

   [30 marks] AO4 [4 marks]

Five key stages to follow

1. **Read** the **question**; **highlight** key words.
2. **Read** the **passage** with the **key words** from the **question** in mind.
3. Quickly **generate ideas** for your response.
4. **Plan** for paragraphs.
5. **Write** your response; **check it** against your plan as you progress.

What do I focus on?

Highlight the **key words**:

4. Starting with this conversation, explore how Shakespeare presents appearance and reality in *Macbeth*.
   Write about:
   - how Shakespeare presents appearance and reality in this extract
   - how Shakespeare presents appearance and reality in the play as a whole.

What do they tell you? Focus on both extract and whole text; explain what specific methods Shakespeare uses; stick to appearance and reality as main topic.

How should I read the passage?

- Check for any immediate links to the question (e.g. Lady Macbeth uses **euphemistic** language).
- Look for any evidence/quotations you could highlight (e.g. **'look like th'innocent flower'**).

How do I get my ideas?

Note your ideas in a spider diagram or list them in a table:

The extract

Lady Macbeth's euphemistic language – 'provided for', 'great business'

Lady Macbeth's simile – 'look like th'innocent flower'

Appearance and reality

The play as a whole

Ambiguous language of witches' prophecies develops this theme

Macbeth realises witches' language tricked him (Act V)

The extract	The play as a whole
● Lady Macbeth uses euphemistic language to mask murder, such as 'provided for' and 'great business' ● Lady Macbeth's simile illustrates this theme – 'look like th'innocent flower'	● Witches' prophecies use ambiguous language to mask truth in Acts I and IV ● Macbeth realises the witches' language deceived him

How do I structure my ideas?

Make a **plan** for **paragraphs**.* Decide the order for your points:

● Paragraph 1: Go straight into your first point: *Secret conversation – in this scene, Lady Macbeth tells Macbeth to hide his evil intentions.*

● Paragraph 2: *In this scene, Lady Macbeth uses a simile to illustrate her point – 'look like th'innocent flower'.*

● Paragraph 3: *In the extract, Lady Macbeth uses euphemisms to mask murder. Earlier 'Not so happy' masks Banquo's death.*

● Paragraph 4: *Lady Macbeth plans the concealment – after Duncan's murder in Act II, Macbeth seems more skilled at hiding his guilt – later, from Act III onwards, he hides his evil intentions from his wife too.*

● Paragraph 5: *Throughout the play, the witches' ambiguous language illustrates Shakespeare's theme of appearance and reality.*

How do I write effectively?

Write **clear**, **analytical** paragraphs and **embed** your evidence fluently, e.g.:

In the extract, Lady Macbeth encourages Macbeth to mask his evil intentions by playing the role of a welcoming host. Shakespeare presents the theme of appearance and reality by using natural imagery which is seen when Lady Macbeth tells Macbeth to 'look like th'innocent flower/But be the serpent under't'. These contradictory images remind us of the witches' chant 'Fair is foul' from the start of the play since a flower is pleasant or 'fair' but a poisonous serpent signals evil.	Overview point – extract Key term Quotations are embedded in the sentence Link to rest of play Summary point

Now you try!

Re-read Question 5 on page 73 and plan your response in the same way.

* The plan above and the sample answers have five paragraphs but you don't need to be limited to this if you have more points to include.

What does a Grade 5 answer look like?

Read the task again, then the sample answer below.

4. Starting with this conversation, explore how Shakespeare presents appearance and reality in *Macbeth*.

Write about:

- how Shakespeare presents appearance and reality in this extract
- how Shakespeare presents appearance and reality in the play as a whole.

[30 marks] AO4 [4 marks]

In the passage Macbeth and Lady Macbeth are having a secret conversation about how to hide their plan to murder King Duncan. Lady Macbeth is worried that Macbeth will give the game away when she says, 'Your face, my thane, is as a book'. The use of the word 'book' means something to read so this shows that she reckons King Duncan might read Macbeth's evil thoughts in his face. That is why she is telling Macbeth to disguise them.

> **AO1** Clear statement setting out viewpoint

> **AO2** Close reference to word use and what it means, if rather informal

Lady Macbeth uses a simile to explain what she means when she says Macbeth needs to be 'like th'innocent flower' but hide a 'serpent' underneath. A 'flower' looks pleasant and this shows us that she wants Macbeth to be friendly when he greets King Duncan, and I think Duncan would trust this sort of a greeting because at the start of the play Macbeth was loyal to the king but now he isn't and wants to kill him. Lady Macbeth wants Macbeth to hide his murder plan like a serpent that is hiding underneath a flower.

> **AO1** Clear progression to next point

> **AO4** Rather a long, awkward sentence

Another way this theme is shown is by the language that Lady Macbeth uses. When she says that Duncan will be 'provided for' this means more than one thing. It reminds me of how the witches hide Banquo's future death by what they say to him in Act I Scene 3 which seems confusing in the same way.

> **AO2** This doesn't add anything as no analysis

> **AO2** Tries to explain idea but doesn't develop sufficiently

When Lady Macbeth says 'look up clear', she wants Macbeth to put on an honest expression during King Duncan's visit; it was common for Jacobean noblemen to entertain each other at their castles and Lady Macbeth wants Macbeth to act as a welcoming host so she gives him instructions. Later, Macbeth starts hiding his own evil when he pretends to be upset by King Duncan's murder. Then, in Act III, he even hides the truth from Lady Macbeth when he says 'Be innocent' about his plan to murder Banquo.

— Paragraph 4

The witches' language is ambiguous throughout the play, such as 'Fair is foul' meaning that nothing is what it seems. When they suggest that Macbeth will become king, he plans Duncan's murder but they never said kill anyone. Later, they speak in riddles such as telling Macbeth he won't be harmed by any man born of a woman; this seems impossible but it comes true in Act V when Macduff says he was ripped from the womb. This means that the witches' language tricked Macbeth which is why he calls them 'juggling fiends'.

— Paragraph 5

Check the skills

Re-read paragraphs four and five of this response and:

- Highlight other **points** made
- Circle any reference to **context**
- Underline any places where the student has made an **interpretation**

Now you try!

Look again at paragraph three ('*Another way this theme is shown is by the language*', etc.) and improve it by:

- Adding a **reference or quotation** which shows how the witches refer to Banquo's death in Act I Scene 3 and **explaining** why it masks the truth
- **Explaining** why the words **'provided for'** are a euphemism for murder
- Ending with a **summary point** about language with double meanings and why this is significant
- Improving the overall **style** by making sure your sentences **flow**; using connectives to **link** ideas

What does a Grade 7+ answer look like?

Read the task again, then the sample answer below.

4. Starting with this conversation, explore how Shakespeare presents appearance and reality in *Macbeth*.

Write about:

● how Shakespeare presents appearance and reality in this extract

● how Shakespeare presents appearance and reality in the play as a whole.

[30 marks] AO4 [4 marks]

In this passage Shakespeare uses the Macbeths' secret conversation about concealment to explore his theme of appearance and reality. Prior to this scene, the couple have both had murderous thoughts and here these thoughts become words, although their evil is masked by euphemisms. Lady Macbeth warns Macbeth that his face can be 'read' like a 'book'. This simile warns that unguarded facial expressions can expose evil intentions. As the play progresses Macbeth becomes more accomplished in the art of disguise, but here his wife is the expert.

Shakespeare illustrates this theme through natural imagery when Lady Macbeth urges Macbeth to 'look like th'innocent flower' but to be 'the serpent under't'. Here Shakespeare may have been alluding to the Bible story of the Garden of Eden where a snake tempts Eve to eat forbidden fruit. Lady Macbeth's simile therefore associates the snake with murderous thoughts, while the 'innocent flower' represents the pleasant façade that she wishes to present to King Duncan.

Shakespeare's euphemistic language in this passage suggests concealment. When Lady Macbeth says King Duncan must be 'provided for', her words could be about preparing food, but they are actually a euphemism for murder. This masked reference to death could be linked to Act I Scene 3 where the witches tell Banquo that he will be 'Not so happy' as Macbeth, since their words could refer to his murder.

AO1 Clear statement sets out argument

AO2 Immediate structural link made with evidence to earlier part of play

AO1 Point is developed and interpreted

AO1 Excellent summary of overall argument

AO3 Excellent knowledge of context linked to Shakespeare's viewpoint

AO2 Carefully selected evidence and detailed analysis of language use and effect

AO1 Fluent introduction of new aspect to analyse

AO4 Uses sophisticated vocabulary

In Jacobean times it would have been an honour to receive a visit from the king. Therefore, Lady Macbeth instructs Macbeth about how to perform as the perfect host. However, as the play progresses, Macbeth becomes skilled at concealing his own crimes. For example, he uses gushing phrases such as 'silver skin lac'd with his golden blood' to suggest outrage after Duncan's murder. From Act III onwards, he acts independently by concealing further murder plans even from his wife.

— Paragraph 4

Throughout the play, Shakespeare uses the witches' ambiguous language such as 'Fair is foul' to imply that nothing is what it seems. The witches never tell Macbeth to kill anyone, but their suggestion that he will be 'king hereafter' tempts him into regicide. Later, he believes he has a 'charmed life' after hearing the witches say he cannot be harmed by man born of woman. This false confidence is shattered when Macduff reveals that he was born by caesarean. Finally, Macbeth refers to the witches as 'juggling fiends', implying that he realises their ambiguous language tricked him.

— Paragraph 5

Check the skills

Re-read paragraphs four and five of this response and:

- Identify any particularly **fluent** or **well-expressed** ideas
- Find any further references to **context**
- Highlight any places where the student has shown **deeper insight** and offered **original** or particularly **thoughtful** ideas or made interesting **links**

Now you try!

Now, using the plan you made for Question 5 on page 75, write a full response. Here's a reminder of the question:

5. Starting with this conversation, explore how Shakespeare presents the supernatural in *Macbeth*.

  Write about:

   - how Shakespeare presents the supernatural in this conversation
   - how Shakespeare presents the supernatural in the play as a whole.

   [30 marks] AO4 [4 marks]

- Try to match your answer to the High Level objectives on page 63.

Now you try!

Now, apply the skills you have learned to these two new questions:

- Note down key points from the extract.
- Select the key quotations you want to use from the extract.
- Repeat the process with other ideas from the play as a whole.
- Write your answer.
- Look at the suggested list of key points in the **Answers** (page 88).

Read this extract from Act IV Scene 3 and answer the question that follows.

In this scene Malcolm and Macduff plan an attack on Macbeth's castle.

> **MALCOLM**
> Be this the whetstone of your sword, let grief
> Covert to anger. Blunt not the heart, enrage it.
>
> **MACDUFF**
> O, I could play the woman with mine eyes
> And braggart with my tongue. But gentle heavens,
> 235 Cut short all intermission. Front to front
> Bring thou this fiend of Scotland and myself;
> Within my sword's length set him. If he scape,
> Heaven forgive him too.
>
> **MALCOLM**
>   This tune goes manly.
> Come, go we to the king; our power is ready;
> 240 Our lack is nothing but our leave. Macbeth
> Is ripe for the shaking, and the powers above
> Put on their instruments. Receive what cheer you may:

6. Starting with this conversation, explore how Shakespeare presents revenge in *Macbeth*.

   Write about:
   - how revenge is presented in this extract
   - how revenge is presented in the play as a whole.

   [30 marks] AO4 [4 marks]

Read this extract from Act IV Scene 3 and answer the question that follows.

At this point in the play Ross has just told Macduff that his wife and children have been murdered.

> **MACDUFF**
> My children too?
>
> **ROSS**
>   Wife, children, servants, all
> That could be found.
>
> **MACDUFF**
>   And I must be from thence?
> 215 My wife kill'd too?
>
> **ROSS**
>   I have said.
>
> **MALCOM**
>   Be comforted
> Let's make us med'cines of our great revenge
> To cure this deadly grief.
>
> **MACDUFF**
> He has no children. All my pretty ones?
> Did you say all? O hell-kite! All?
> 220 What, all my pretty chickens and their dam
> At one fell swoop?
>
> **MALCOLM**
> Dispute it like a man.
>
> **MACDUFF**
> I shall do so;
> But I must also feel it as a man;

7. Starting with this conversation, explain explore how Shakespeare presents the relationship between Macduff and his family.

   Write about:

   - how Shakespeare presents the relationship between Macduff and his family in this extract
   - how Shakespeare presents the relationship between Macduff and his family in the play as a whole.

   [30 marks] AO4 [4 marks]

GLOSSARY

Literary or language terms	Explanation
adjective	a word used to describe something or somebody (e.g. the *red* hat)
aside	something said by a character, which is intended to be heard by the audience but not by the other characters on the stage
blank verse	unrhymed lines in iambic pentameter (lines consisting of five iambs each – each iamb made up of a weak syllable followed by a strong one)
dramatic irony	when the audience can see more significance in the words of a character than the characters in the play can
enjambment	in poetry when a line runs on into the next line without pause, so carrying the thought with it. Sometimes called a run-on line.
euphemism	a word or phrase that is mild and less blunt than the actual subject
foreshadowing	a hint of what is to come in a work of poetry, fiction or drama
imagery	descriptive language that uses images to make actions, objects and characters more vivid in the reader's mind
irony	deliberately saying one thing when you mean another, usually in a humorous, sarcastic or sometimes thoughtful way
juxtaposition	two ideas, images or objects positioned close together to highlight their differences
metaphor	when one thing is used to describe another to create a striking or unusual image
motif	an image, idea or situation that recurs throughout the text, forming a pattern
personification	the treatment or description of an object or idea as though they have human feelings and attributes
prose	a form of language that has the natural flow of speech, rather than poetry, which has a rhythmic structure
protagonist	the main or a major character
rhetorical question	a question asked for effect rather than for an answer
rhyming couplet	a couplet (two paired lines) that rhymes
setting	the place or environment where the events in a story are set
simile	when one thing is compared directly with another using 'like' or 'as'
soliloquy	a dramatic technique that allows a character to make a speech as if thinking aloud, revealing their inner thoughts to the audience
stage directions	advice printed in the text of a play, giving instructions or information to the actors, or on setting and special effects
subplot	a secondary storyline that supports the main one, often by reinforcing the theme
symbol	something that represents something else, usually with meanings that are widely known, e.g. a dove as a symbol of peace
theme	a recurrent idea in a work of literature
tragedy	a form of classical drama associated with the Ancient Greeks and Romans, in which the protagonist's fatal flaw results in his downfall

ANSWERS

Note that the sample paragraphs given here provide only one possible approach to each task. Many other approaches would also be valid and appropriate.

PLOT AND STRUCTURE

Act I Scenes 1-4 - Now you try! (page 5)

Shakespeare also reveals other aspects of Macbeth's character in the early scenes of Act I. One of these is his evil side which is evident in Act I Scene 5 when he mentions 'black and deep desires'. These words refer to the idea of murdering King Duncan in order to become king. Macbeth does not want 'light' to see such thoughts because light represents goodness and he wants to keep his evil thoughts hidden.

Act I Scenes 5-7 - Now you try! (page 7)

Shakespeare further explores the concept of evil in the second half of Act I when Lady Macbeth calls on 'spirits' to fill her with 'direst cruelty'. By calling on such spirits Lady Macbeth associates herself with the witches. She also uses the superlative adjective 'direst' to suggest that she hopes to be capable of extreme cruelty: she wants to become evil enough to persuade Macbeth to murder King Duncan.

Act II - Now you try! (page 9)

Another important motif in Act II is blood. In Act II Scene 2 Macbeth says 'Will all great Neptune's ocean wash this blood/Clean from my hand', suggesting that his guilt can never be removed. Shakespeare associates the motif of blood with guilt throughout the play. In Act V, when Lady Macbeth is sleepwalking, she imagines there is blood on her hands that she cannot wash away.

Act III Scenes 1-3 - Now you try! (page 11)

Macbeth's concerns about Banquo also change early in Act III. This is evident when Macbeth claims 'For Banquo's issue have I fil'd my mind;/For them, the gracious Duncan have I murder'd', suggesting that he fears that Banquo's descendants will become kings and that he has committed a terrible crime for their benefit. His repetition of the word 'for' builds up emotional tension, suggesting that he feels angry or distressed.

Act III Scenes 4-6 - Now you try! (page 13)

However, Macbeth believes that the ghost is real and he is terrified of it. This is seen when he tells it: 'never shake/Thy gory locks at me!' The exclamation mark suggests strong emotion and the word 'gory' implies that the ghost looks gruesome. Macbeth gives all his attention to the ghost rather than to his guests, implying he is barely aware of his circumstances when it is present.

Act IV - Now you try! (page 15)

Shakespeare also uses the image of a stormy sea to depict the state of Scotland under Macbeth's leadership.

This is evident when Ross implies that the Scottish people 'float upon a wild and violent sea'. The adjectives 'wild' and 'violent' suggest something dangerous, which may be why Ross links this image to feelings of fear. His image also reminds us of the witches' talk of creating a tempest at sea in Act I Scene 3.

Act V - Now you try! (page 17)

After Lady Macbeth dies, Macbeth believes that life is meaningless. This is evident when he compares it to a 'brief candle', suggesting that a person's life force burns out quickly. He also compares life to an actor who 'struts' on a stage for a short time. The verb 'struts' suggests that he believes life is a mere performance which has little significance and is quickly ended.

Form and Structure - Now you try! (page 19)

When Macbeth hears the apparitions' Act IV predictions he feels confident of success but they foreshadow his downfall. This is evident when Macduff kills him in Act V Scene 8. In Act IV the witches tell Macbeth to 'beware Macduff' and to be wary of man not born of woman. Macbeth dismisses the latter as unlikely, but in Act V Macduff reveals that he was 'Untimely ripp'd' from his mother's womb, thus fulfilling the prophecy.

Quick revision - Quick quiz (page 20)

1. Stormy   2. The Captain   3. He is executed for treason.   4. Banquo's descendants will be kings.
5. His son, Malcolm   6. A dagger   7. Macduff
8. The grooms   9. Because they are afraid they may be killed like their father   10. Fleance
11. In Macbeth's place   12. Hecate
13. To warn them that they are in danger   14. Ross
15. The Doctor and a Gentlewoman
16. Malcolm's men cut down branches from Birnam Wood as camouflage.   17. Young Siward
18. Malcolm   19. Ambition   20. The banquet scene (Act III Scene 4)

Quick revision - Power paragraphs (page 21)

1. Macbeth and Banquo respond to the witches very differently in Act I. Initially, Macbeth seems to fear them whereas Banquo claims that he is not frightened of their 'favours' or their 'hate'. Both men receive promises related to kingship but Banquo views these with suspicion, believing that the witches' words could be dangerous, while Macbeth starts thinking about committing murder to remove the obstacles in his path to kingship.
2. The discussion breaks the tension after King Duncan's murder; it encourages the audience to reflect upon the consequences of regicide. It also suggests the natural world has been disrupted, e.g. a 'mousing owl' killing a 'falcon'. These birds might represent Macbeth and King Duncan and the Great Chain of Being, as a falcon is usually more powerful.

ANSWERS

Quick revision – Exam practice (page 21)

- When Macduff defeats and kills Macbeth, he fulfils the witches' prophecy; Macduff is presented as an instrument of justice; he is supporting the rightful heir against a usurper; Macbeth is linked to evil when Macduff addresses him as a 'hell-hound'; this scene develops Shakespeare's theme of betrayal and revenge.
- We learn more about Macbeth; he dismisses the Roman tradition of committing suicide rather than surrendering; he draws false confidence from the witches' predictions and claims to have a 'charmed life'; his confidence is shaken when Macduff reveals that he was born by caesarean, fulfilling the witches' prophecy.

SETTING AND CONTEXT

Jacobean society – Now you try! (page 23)

In Jacobean times many people believed that witches could vanish into thin air. This power is seen in the play when Macbeth says, 'what seem'd corporal,/Melted, as breath into the wind'. Shakespeare uses their disappearance to add mystery to the witches because something 'corporal' is solid and therefore it should be impossible for it to melt away. Shakespeare may have included the witches in the play to appeal to James I who had written a book on this subject.

Succession and order – Now you try! (page 25)

Malcolm and his followers want to remove Macbeth from power and restore the rightful monarchy. This is evident when Malcolm claims that 'Macbeth/Is ripe for shaking'. His words suggest that, like a rotten apple, Macbeth is ready to fall. In line with the Jacobean belief that God was on the side of the rightful monarch and would therefore support his cause, Malcolm asks the 'powers above' to 'Put on their instruments'.

Quick revision – Quick quiz (page 27)

1. He was interested in witches and had written a book on the subject.   2. To stay at home and look after the children   3. She persuades Macbeth to kill King Duncan just as Eve persuades Adam to eat the forbidden fruit.   4. They sat according to their ranks.
5. The belief that the king was appointed by God
6. He is reported to have the gifts of prophecy and healing.   7. At Scone   8. The castle seems very pleasant.   9. The scene in which Lady Macduff and her son are attacked by murderers (Act IV Scene 2)
10. Scotland is described as weeping and bleeding.

Quick revision – Power paragraphs (page 27)

a) Shakespeare's theme of evil is illustrated when the porter describes the entrance to the castle as a 'hell-gate' as his words remind us of the horrors that lie within; the castle is the setting for the dramatic events of Act V, such as sleepwalking which reflects the theme of madness and fights which reflect the theme of conflict.

b) Macbeth's castle is a significant setting because much of the action happens there; Duncan says the castle has a 'pleasant seat'; this is dramatic irony as he dies there. Duncan's reaction to the castle suggests that he tends to be too trusting and that he takes things at face value.

CHARACTERS

Macbeth in Acts I and II – Now you try! (page 29)

Macbeth's conscience is also apparent when he refuses to return to the scene of Duncan's murder because he is 'afraid to think what [he has] done'. The audience knows that Macbeth is not frightened of blood, because he 'unseam'd' Macdonald in battle, therefore they might conclude that it is the act of regicide that has frightened Macbeth. This quotation implies that he fears the consequences of his actions.

Macbeth in Acts III–V – Now you try! (page 31)

The audience might also sympathise with Macbeth in Act V when he says he is tied 'to a stake' and 'cannot fly'. This implies that he cannot escape from Malcolm's army but intends to be 'bear-like' and 'fight the course'. His image refers to the popular Jacobean pursuit of bear baiting, which involved a bear being chained to post while dogs tormented it. By using this image Macbeth indicates that he will fight on against the odds.

Lady Macbeth – Now you try! (page 33)

Lady Macbeth's feelings about having bloody hands, which symbolise guilt, change as the play progresses. In Act II, she was sure that 'A little water' would wash away her guilt but in Act V she feels that 'all the perfumes of Arabia' will not sweeten her hand. This suggests that her guilty conscience is troubling her.

Banquo – Now you try! (page 35)

Once Macbeth becomes king, Banquo becomes a threat to him. This is evident when he remembers the witches' promise that Banquo would be 'father to a line of kings', that Banquo's children would eventually take the throne. Macbeth refers to his own crown as 'fruitless' because he has no children. Therefore, he fears that he has murdered King Duncan only to benefit Banquo's descendants.

Macduff and Lady Macduff – Now you try! (page 37)

Macduff is very distressed by the brutal murders of his family. This is evident when he asks if the murderers took 'all my pretty chickens and their dam/At one fell swoop?'. This image is of a predatory bird swooping into a nest and killing the hen and her chicks, which implies that his family were helpless. His distress is also apparent when he keeps questioning Ross, suggesting that he finds it hard to believe the terrible news.

King Duncan and Malcolm – Now you try! (page 39)

Malcolm does not seem to be as trusting as his father. This is evident when he decides to flee from Macbeth's castle after King Duncan's murder because he fears the 'murderous shaft that's shot/Hath not yet lighted'. This image of an arrow that has not yet hit its target suggests that he believes whoever murdered Duncan might be about to strike again.

The witches – Now you try! (page 41)

Shakespeare also makes the witches sound mysterious when they speak in rhyming couplets. When they are mixing their potion, they chant 'Double, double toil and trouble;/Fire burn, and cauldron bubble'. These words create a magical atmosphere. The negative implications of the words 'toil' and 'trouble' suggest evil and since the witches repeat these words several times, speaking chorally, the audience gets the impression that this rhyming couplet is needed to cast the spell.

Quick revision – Quick quiz (page 42)

1. Banquo   2. Bravery/courage   3. Lady Macbeth
4. Macduff   5. Banquo   6. He is afraid to think about what he has done or see the crime scene again.
7. Some people believe that the Hecate scenes were not written by Shakespeare.   8. She feels he was unwise to leave them.   9. He fears Banquo's descendants may take his throne.   10. She probably kills herself.   11. One   12. Macbeth   13. The witches   14. Because he looked like her father   15. They put them in their cauldron.   16. Macbeth's coronation and banquet   17. Imaginary blood
18. By caesarean section   19. Act I Scene 1, Act I Scene 3, Act III Scene 5, Act IV Scene 1   20. Macbeth

Quick revision – Power paragraphs (page 43)

1. Lady Macduff's murder acts as a trigger for Malcolm's army to attack Macbeth; it shows how evil Macbeth has become as his only justification for killing her was that he had been told to 'beware Macduff'.
2. This scene develops the theme of the supernatural; the hideous ingredients such as the finger of a 'birth-strangl'd babe' emphasise the witches' evil. The chanting of 'Double, double toil and trouble' gives the scene a magical atmosphere.

Quick revision – Exam practice (page 43)

- Lady Macbeth claims that alcohol has made her 'bold' but her behaviour seems anxious; Shakespeare indicates her agitation when she is startled by the noise of an owl's cry and exclaims, 'Hark, peace!'; this short, exclamatory sentence suggests she is trying to calm her nerves.
- Shakespeare also portrays Lady Macbeth's nervousness when she worries that the murder plan might have failed; although she drugged the grooms she feels afraid that 'they have awak'd'; this fear contrasts her confidence earlier in the play when she told Macbeth that they would not fail; she seems

vulnerable when she says she could not murder King Duncan because he looked like her father.

Ambition – Now you try! (page 45)

Shakespeare also reveals Macbeth's ambition when he claims that his only reason for murdering King Duncan is 'Vaulting ambition'. The word 'vaulting' has associations of jumping or leaping and reminds us of his desire to 'o'erleap' Malcolm. In both instances, Macbeth wants to move up in the order of the succession, even if he has to kill to do this.

Betrayal and revenge – Now you try! (page 47)

Shakespeare also suggests that Malcolm's revenge could heal Scotland. This is evident when Malcolm suggests that his army can make 'med'cines of our great revenge'. Medicines are used to cure illness, so he is implying that his forces can heal Scotland's wounds. Furthermore, he speaks of curing 'this deadly grief'. This image is associated with the sadness that Macbeth has caused both Macduff and Scotland.

The supernatural – Now you try! (page 49)

The witches are also presented as evil when Macbeth calls the air on which they ride 'Infected'. This word is associated with contagious diseases so he is implying that their evil could spread. He also claims that those who trust them are 'damn'd'. This is an example of dramatic irony, because the witches' evil contributes to his downfall and death.

Fate and free will – Now you try! (page 51)

Macbeth also seems to make a clear decision to murder Banquo's son, Fleance. This is evident when Macbeth tells the murderers that Fleance should 'embrace the fate/Of that dark hour'. He believes he is taking control of fate in order to overcome the witches' prediction that Banquo's sons will be king. He refers to the moment of murder as a 'dark hour', associating darkness with evil as happens throughout the play.

Appearance and reality – Now you try! (page 53)

Shakespeare also shows characters deliberately hiding their true thoughts or intentions. This is seen when Lady Macbeth tells Macbeth to look like 'th'innocent flower,/But be the serpent under't'. The contrasting images of a beautiful flower and a poisonous snake are used to encourage Macbeth to look welcoming on the outside, while masking thoughts of murder. A snake also has literary associations of evil.

Guilt and madness – Now you try! (page 55)

Shakespeare reveals that Macbeth's mind is disturbed when he tells his wife 'Methought I heard a voice cry, "Sleep no more"' after he murders King Duncan. The function of sleep is to soothe the body and mind, so without it, Macbeth is likely to suffer mentally and physically. His use of the word 'methought' suggests he may have imagined the voice and that it could therefore be a product of his guilt.

Quick revision – Quick quiz (page 56)

1. The witches   2. They don't tell Macbeth to commit a crime.   3. King Duncan naming Malcolm as the heir to his throne   4. Banquo hopes his descendants will become kings.   5. Ambition   6. Those who betray others often hide their intentions, e.g. Lady Macbeth pretends to be a welcoming hostess when she is planning King Duncan's murder.   7. The Thane of Cawdor   8. Fate   9. Lady Macbeth   10. Macbeth actively seeks out the witches in Act IV whereas his meeting with them in Act I was not planned.
11. The murders of his family   12. Distressed   13. Malcolm's army is reinforced by nobles who used to support Macbeth.   14. A light   15. He is terrified.   16. To 'beware Macduff' and 'none of woman born/ Shall harm Macbeth'   17. Because only Macbeth can see Banquo's ghost   18. Blood and water   19. When he appears as an apparition (Act IV Scene 1)   20. serpent

Quick revision – Power paragraphs (page 57)

1. The witches appear in thunder and lightning, weather conditions often associated with evil; speaking in rhyming couplets and sometimes chorally makes them sound magical; they refer to their familiars: a cat, 'Greymalkin' and a toad 'Paddock'; familiars were believed to be spirits in animal form that accompanied and assisted witches.
2. Shakespeare uses sleeplessness as a sign of guilt in the play: both Macbeth and his wife suffer from disturbed sleep as a result of their crimes; after Macbeth kills King Duncan he fears he won't sleep peacefully again; when Lady Macbeth sleepwalks, the doctor says 'More needs she the divine than the physician', suggesting that her sleeplessness is a symptom of her guilt.

Quick revision – Exam practice (page 57)

- Banquo seems concerned that Macbeth played 'foully' to achieve his ambition of becoming king; unlike any other character, he is aware of the witches' predictions for Macbeth; his use of the word 'foully' implies wrongdoing, suggesting that he believes it is wrong to commit crimes in order to gain power.
- Banquo clearly has his own ambitions; he spends the majority of this speech reflecting on his own circumstances rather than Macbeth's; he dwells on the witches' promise that he will be 'the root and father' of many kings; unlike Macbeth, Banquo silences his ambitious thoughts when he says, 'hush, no more'. This could be because he thinks his ambitions are dangerous.

LANGUAGE

Imagery and symbolism – Now you try! (page 59)

Shakespeare uses a metaphor to suggest that it was wrong to steal Duncan's throne when in Act V Angus refers to Macbeth as a 'dwarfish thief' in a 'giant's robe'. This image of a 'thief' suggests that Macbeth has stolen Duncan's title and the adjective 'dwarfish' suggests that he is less important than Duncan, the rightful monarch, who is presented as a 'giant' because of his importance.

Dramatic techniques – Now you try! (page 61)

Shakespeare also uses sound to build tension when his characters hear strange noises at dramatic points in the play. For example, when Lady Macbeth is waiting for Macbeth to return from murdering King Duncan she hears 'the owl scream and the crickets cry'. The words 'scream' and 'cry' create images of pain which could be associated with Duncan's murder and owls are predatory birds that attack at night, linking them with Macbeth.

EXAM PRACTICE

Planning your character response – Now you try! (page 67)

- **Paragraph 1**: In this passage, Duncan realises that he misjudged the first Thane of Cawdor yet in Act I he misjudges the Macbeths as hosts.
- **Paragraph 2**: In this extract, Duncan expresses his gratitude for Macbeth's support, but later risks losing Macbeth's loyalty when he names Malcolm as his successor.
- **Paragraph 3**: In this scene, Macbeth's long sentence and use of enjambment indicates that he is lying – but Duncan is not suspicious, unlike his sons later.
- **Paragraph 4**: In the extract, Duncan accepts Macbeth's claims of owing duties to 'throne … children and servants' but in Act II, Macbeth murders him.
- **Paragraph 5**: In this passage, both men use financial terms, e.g. 'pays' – it seems Duncan has to buy love – in Act II Duncan pays with his life.

Grade 5 answer – Check the skills (page 69)

- **Points:** It seems as though Macbeth is not frightened because he has done too many evil things; When Macbeth hears the cry he remembers a time when a noise like that would have scared him.
- **Context:** In Shakespeare's day they did not have much scenery, so noises like this were used to build up tension.
- **Interpretation:** I think he was a better person when he did feel some fear after killing Duncan and Banquo because this showed that he had a conscience; At that time he was more fearful and I think it was because he felt guilty but now he has lost his guilt so he has also lost his fear.

Grade 5 answer – Now you try! (page 69)

When Macbeth says 'I have almost forgot the taste of fears', Shakespeare suggests that he has lost the sensory capacity to feel fear. This fearlessness seems very different from his behaviour in other scenes in the play, for example, when he sees Banquo's ghost he shouts 'Hence horrible shadow', suggesting that he is terrified of it. Shakespeare implies that although Macbeth can remember the feeling of fear, he can no longer experience it.

Grade 7+ answer - Check the skills (page 71)

- **Fluent or well-expressed ideas:** Shakespeare also suggests that Macbeth feels little fear because he has 'supp'd full with horrors', suggesting that his unnatural deeds have numbed his natural responses; These words remind us of the 'horrible imaginings' which he claimed 'unfix[ed]' his hair as he contemplated King Duncan's murder.
- **Context:** In Shakespeare's time, there was little scenery, so sound effects were used to build up tension.
- **Deeper insight/thoughtful ideas:** it could be argued that if Macbeth had allowed himself to feel more fear, he might not have ended up in such a dangerous situation since this fear might have prevented him from committing regicide; It is possible that he killed his capacity to fear when he stopped listening to his conscience.

Grade 7+ answer - Now you try! (page 71)

AO1

- In this passage, Duncan realises he misjudged the first Thane of Cawdor, but later he completely misjudges the Macbeths when they act as hosts.
- In the same scene, he describes the Macbeths' castle as pleasant, not knowing he will die there.
- In the extract, Duncan expresses his gratitude for Macbeth's support but later risks losing Macbeth's loyalty by naming Malcolm as successor.
- In this passage, Duncan takes Macbeth's gushing words at face value. He seems more trusting than his sons are after Duncan's death.
- In the extract, Macbeth says he owes duties to Duncan's 'throne and state, children and servants' but in Act II he murders Duncan.

AO2

- In Act I, Shakespeare uses the story of the first Thane of Cawdor to foreshadow the fact that Macbeth will betray Duncan.
- In this passage, Shakespeare uses enjambment in Macbeth's sentence beginning 'The service and loyalty I owe' to suggest Macbeth is gushing but Duncan trusts him.
- In this extract, both men use the financial terms like 'pays' to suggest loyalty should be rewarded. It seems Duncan has to buy love, which should make him less trusting.
- There is also irony in Duncan's words 'More is thy due than more than all can pay' because Duncan pays the ultimate price – his life.

AO3

- There were plots against King James I's throne in Shakespeare's time, so for Duncan to be so trusting is perhaps naive.
- In Shakespeare's day, the king would reward loyal subjects with titles, such as Macbeth's title, Thane of Cawdor.

Planning your theme response - Now you try! (page 75)

- **Paragraph 1:** In this extract, Shakespeare raises questions about the reality of the ghost – like the dagger in Act II – as only Macbeth sees it.
- **Paragraph 2:** Shakespeare uses supernatural scenes to add mystery, e.g. first appearance of witches in Act I – audience wonder who or what they are.
- **Paragraph 3:** Supernatural appearances evoke fear. In this passage, Macbeth is very frightened by the ghost. He is also distressed by the apparition of Banquo's ghost in Act IV.
- **Paragraph 4:** In this scene, Macbeth breaks out of iambic pentameter in the line starting 'Prithee, see there!'. Throughout the play the witches do not speak in iambic pentameter.
- **Paragraph 5:** The supernatural evokes horror as Macbeth conveys his dread using the image of the dead returning from graves. The witches' language in Act IV also conjures up horrific images.couplets to make them sound magical.

Grade 5 answer - Check the skills (page 77)

- **Points:** she wants Macbeth to put on an honest expression during King Duncan's visit; Later, Macbeth starts hiding his own evil
- **Context:** it was common for Jacobean noblemen to entertain each other at their castles
- **Interpretation:** Macbeth starts hiding his own evil when he pretends to be upset by King Duncan's murder; he even hides the truth from Lady Macbeth when he says 'Be innocent' about his plan to murder Banquo; The witches' language is ambiguous throughout the play, such as 'Fair is foul' meaning that nothing is what it seems.

Grade 5 answer - Now you try! (page 77)

Another way that Shakespeare develops his theme of appearance and reality is through Lady Macbeth's language. When she says that Duncan will be 'provided for' this could refer to gathering food or drink for his visit, but her true meaning is killing him. This euphemistic language resembles the way the witches play with words. For example, when they say that Banquo will be 'lesser' than Macbeth, they could mean that he will die. Shakespeare uses language with double meanings throughout the play to allow characters to mask their intentions, which adds tension to the play.

Grade 7+ answer - Check the skills (page 79)

- **Fluent or well-expressed ideas:** Therefore, Lady Macbeth instructs Macbeth about how about how to perform as the perfect host; as the play progresses, Macbeth becomes skilled at concealing his own crimes.
- **Context:** In Jacobean times it would have been an honour to receive a visit from the king.
- **Deeper insight/thoughtful ideas:** The witches never tell Macbeth to kill anyone, but their suggestion that he will be 'king hereafter' tempts him into regicide.

ANSWERS

Grade 7+ answer – Now you try! (page 79)

AO1
- In this scene, Shakespeare raises questions about the reality of the ghost as only Macbeth sees it. This question is also raised by the dagger in Act I, but the witches are seen by Banquo too.
- Supernatural appearances can create fear and horror. In this passage, Macbeth is horrified. He is equally distressed by the apparition of Banquo's ghost in Act IV.
- Shakespeare uses supernatural scenes to add mystery and drama to the play. The first appearance of the witches in Act I makes the audience wonder who they are.
- Shakespeare suggests that supernatural forces create disorder. Macbeth disrupts the decorum of the banquet when he sees the ghost. In Act II, nature is disrupted when an owl kills a falcon.

AO2
- In this passage, Lady Macbeth uses short, exclamatory sentences such as 'O proper stuff!' to express scorn.
- In this scene, Macbeth breaks out of iambic pentameter when he says 'Prithee, see there! Behold, look, ho! How say you?', suggesting a loss of control. The witches do not speak in iambic pentameter – their lines are often seven or eight syllables long. Rhyming couplets make them sound magical.
- In this passage, Macbeth conveys horror by using images of bodies rising from graves. The witches' language in Act IV such as 'finger of birth-strangl'd babe' conjures up equally horrific images.

AO3
- Many people in Shakespeare's time, including James I, were interested in the supernatural. Supernatural scenes could have been written to appeal to him.
- Royal banquets were important state occasions and it was inappropriate to interrupt them.

Practice questions – Question 6 (page 80)

AO1
- In this extract, Malcolm urges Macduff to convert his grief about the loss of his family to anger to fuel their revenge. In Act V their army attacks Macbeth's castle to make this revenge a reality.
- In the passage, revenge is presented as violent conflict – only physical, 'manly' action will do. Such violence is seen in Act V when Macduff claims his 'voice is in' his sword before he fights and kills Macbeth.
- Macbeth may have arranged Banquo's murder because Banquo wanted to keep his 'allegiance clear' in Act II Scene 1.
- Macbeth persuades the murderers to kill Banquo by suggesting that it was Banquo who prevented their progress.

AO2
- In this extract, both men use religious language to suggest that they believe God supports their revenge.

- In the passage, Macduff calls Macbeth a 'fiend' which links him with evil spirits and in Act V he calls him a 'hell-hound'. This then indicates that the revenge is moral.
- In this extract, 'ripe for the shaking' suggests that Macbeth is like a rotten fruit ready to fall. The verb 'shaking' refers to Malcolm's army attacking Macbeth's castle to avenge his crimes.
- In this passage, 'Front to front/Bring thou this fiend of Scotland and myself' foreshadows the moment when Macduff confronts Macbeth in Act V.

AO3
- A whetstone was a fine-grained stone which Jacobeans used to sharpen swords and knives.
- Jacobeans believed in the divine right of kings, which states that the king is appointed by God, so Malcolm, the rightful heir, expected God to support his revenge.

Practice questions – Question 7 (page 81)

AO1
- In this extract, Macduff grieves deeply for his family, suggesting he loves them. He tells Ross and Malcolm that he needs to 'feel it as a man'.
- Earlier in Act IV, Lady Macduff appears angry when Macduff leaves her unprotected with the children.
- In Act IV we learn that Macduff has gone to England, suggesting that he chose to defend his country rather than stay with his family.
- Later in this scene, Ross and Malcolm try to convert Macduff's distress to anger. In Act V Macduff suggests that the ghosts of his family will haunt him until he avenges their deaths.

AO2
- In this extract, Shakespeare uses a series of questions to indicate Macduff's disbelief.
- Macduff uses the image of a hen and her chicks to represent his innocent family.
- Earlier in Act IV, Lady Macduff also uses the image of a wren trying to protect her nest from an owl.
- In this passage, Macduff uses a rhetorical question, 'And I must be from thence?' to reprimand himself for leaving his defenceless family.

AO3
- A Jacobean man's role included both protecting his family and fighting for his country. Macduff seems to regret leaving his family to avenge Scotland.
- Shakespeare's audience would expect a wife to fulfil a maternal, loving role like Lady Macduff's.